AUSTRALIAN FOOD & WINE ART

Acknowledgements

The publisher wishes to extend grateful thanks to the chefs and owners
of the restaurants and cafés who supplied recipes
and presented the dishes.

To the artists, galleries and agents who gave permission to reproduce
the wonderful artworks, a special thank you for your generosity.

To our photographer Ian Baker and our design and production staff,
well done and thanks for your enthusiasm.

To Joan Mackenzie at ARW, thanks for your encouragement and support.

Cliff Josephs

Photographs

All photographs are by Ian Baker except for the following:
TRANZ International Image Library: front jacket top and middle right, back jacket bottom left, endpapers (highway to Kings Canyon), p .3, p. 6–7, p. 8–9, p. 14 top, p. 14–15, p. 44–45, p. 48 top, p. 50–51 all, p. 52–53 bottom, p. 56–57, p. 60, p. 64–65, p.72–73 top, p. 76–77 top, p. 92–93, p. 106–107 top, p. 115, p. 154–155, p. 158–159 top, p. 164–165, p. 170–171 left, p. 176–177 top; Vanessa Hunt, Digitello Photography: p. 49, p. 52, p. 55; Kuniya Restaurant: p. 46

Published by Chanel Publishers Ltd in association with Angus & Robertson (Pty) Ltd,
379 Collins Street, Melbourne, VIC 3001

First published by Chanel Publishers Ltd, 2007

Publisher: Cliff Josephs
Photographer: Ian Baker
Text: Vic Williams and Ian Baker
Researcher: Camelia Petrus
Production manager: Barbara Nielsen
Design and layout: Lesley Coomer
Recipe editors: Camelia Petrus and Toni Mason
Map artwork: Pauline Whimp
Indexer: Diane Lowther
Printed by: 1010 Printing International Ltd, Hong Kong

ISBN: 978-0-9582729-3-3

AUSTRALIAN FOOD & WINE ART

Photography: Ian Baker
Text: Vic Williams and Ian Baker

CHANEL

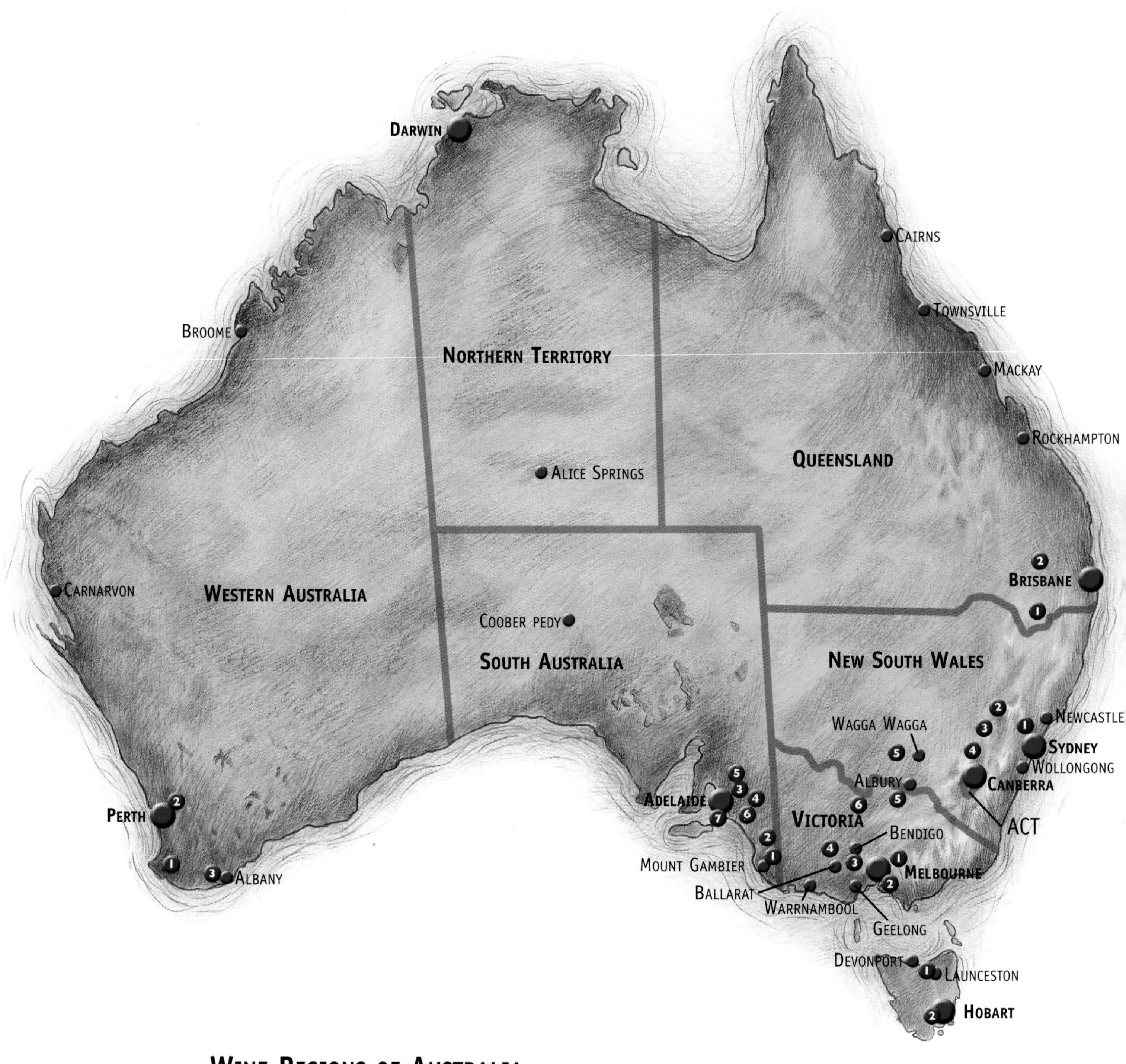

Wine Regions of Australia

Western Australia

1 Margaret River
2 Swan Valley
3 Lower Great Southern

South Australia

1 Coonawarra
2 Padthaway
3 Barossa Valley
4 Eden Valley
5 Clare Valley
6 Adelaide Hills
7 McLaren Vale

Victoria

1 Yarra Valley
2 Mornington Peninsula
3 Macedon Ranges
4 Pyrenees
5 Rutherglen and King Valley
6 Goulburn Valley

Queensland

1 Mt Tamborine
2 Granite Belt

Tasmania

1 Northern Tasmania
2 Southern Tasmania

New South Wales

1 Upper and Lower Hunter Valley
2 Mudgee
3 Orange
4 Cowra

Contents

Introduction

Australia is blessed with a wealth of great food, exciting wines and inspiring art from a number of talented established and emerging artists.

Photographing this richness proved a huge undertaking, but one that was immensely stimulating and rewarding. It was made possible by the unfailingly good-natured co-operation of chefs, winemakers, artists and gallery owners throughout the country, sometimes at a few moments' notice.

We walked the streets of Brisbane, Perth, Adelaide, Hobart, Melbourne, Canberra and Sydney discovering street sculptures and the many other works of art that can be found throughout the land. This proved the best way to get a real feel for the pulsing life of the cities, and to ferret out hidden gems of cafés and restaurants that might otherwise have escaped notice.

We started with an outline of chefs, restaurants and artists gathered from favourable reviews, but we left room for word of mouth recommendations and the inevitable spontaneous finds. There proved to be many, some from a chance cup of coffee and a glance at a previously unknown menu, others from stumbling across a back-street family business serving wonderful food. The end result is a cross-section of the quality and variety of the wonderful food, wine and art available in Australia today.

Our focus has been on regional variation, the ethnic influences of immigrant cultures and the overall 'nowness' of modern Australia. We've concentrated on the major cities and neighbouring areas, but we haven't underestimated the contribution of rural Australia to the quality of life of the entire country in the form of fresh produce, world-beating wines and inspirational local art.

It has been a privilege to work on this book, and I trust that our sampling gives some impression of the vibrance and innovation involved in the food, wine and art of one of the world's great countries.

Ian Baker

Great beaches are
just the beginning
QUEENSLAND

QUEENSLANDERS HAVE EVERY RIGHT to be proud of their state – they really have got the lot! Many visitors head straight for the Gold or Sunshine Coasts, and spend their entire holiday alternating between the golden sand and the azure blue ocean. And that's fine – nothing could be more relaxing or easy on the eye. But there is a great deal more to Queensland than unforgettable beaches.

Up north, where the tropical rainforest meets the Great Barrier Reef and adjacent Whitsunday Islands, the scenery is spectacularly colourful above and below the water. It's a paradise for divers, and offers almost as much excitement for those who prefer to admire the natural world from the comfort of a boat.

The city of Brisbane makes the most of its riverside location with a bevy of restaurants on a wharf that also acts as base for regular ferry trips. Seafood rules, but there are plenty of options for those who prefer land-sourced ingredients.

Queensland is seldom thought of as a wine-making state, but vines have been planted in the major growing region, the Granite Belt, since the 1960s, and a growing number of local labels are well regarded by the pundits. Many wineries welcome tourists, offering well set-up cafés and tasting areas.

Venture inland, and you are likely to find surprises – a determinedly Irish pub in a dusty, classic Australian small town, or food sophistication from a chef taking refuge from the hectic pace of big city kitchens.

Nature offers vivid colour in the so-called sunshine state. We are used to seeing photographs of the bright red, blue and green corals of the reef, but the equally brilliant shades of some rainforest plants often come as a surprise to visitors. Many local artists take their inspiration from this cacophony of colour.

LEFT: North Queensland, where secluded pristine beaches are edged by tropical rainforest.

Chocolate Marquise

in chocolate cups with dragon fruit sherbet and limoncello anglaise

CHOCOLATE CUPS

100g Valrhona white chocolate
250g Valrhona Grand Cru Pur Caraïbe 66% Couverture dark chocolate

Melt the white and the dark chocolate in separate saucepans over a bain-marie. Line 8 muffin cups with non-stick paper cups. Brush a thin layer of white chocolate in a strip down one side, across the bottom and up the other side of each cup, then another strip at 90 degrees to form a cross. Wipe the top edges of each cup and set in the freezer for a minute. Brush the inside of the cups with a layer of dark chocolate, return to the freezer to set and repeat the procedure with a second layer. Peel off the paper and store the chocolate cups in a cool place (not the refrigerator) until needed.

CHOCOLATE MARQUISE

150g Valrhona Grand Cru Pur Caraïbe 66% Couverture chocolate
150g butter
80g sugar
100ml water
2 eggs
2 egg yolks
6 tablespoons cocoa powder
250ml cream

Melt together the chocolate and butter in a saucepan over a bain-marie. In another saucepan, boil the sugar and water for about 5 minutes (soft ball). Beat the eggs and yolks, then pour in the hot liquid sugar and whisk until light and fluffy. Add the cocoa and the melted chocolate mixture and mix well.

Whisk the cream to soft peaks and fold through the chocolate mixture. Spoon the mixture into the chocolate cups and place in a cool room for about 3 hours to set.

LEFT: Brilliantly coloured bromeliads thrive in the tropical warmth of Port Douglas.

DRAGON FRUIT SHERBET

300g (about 4) dragon fruit flesh
200ml water
120g caster sugar
2 tablespoons glucose
grated zest and juice of 1 lime
100ml plain yoghurt

Place the dragon fruit flesh in a bar blender.

In a saucepan, bring the water, sugar and glucose to the boil. Add the lime zest and juice to the dragon fruit, then add the syrup and yoghurt and blend until smooth. Pour into an ice cream maker and freeze.

LIMONCELLO ANGLAISE

125ml milk
125ml cream
6 egg yolks
125g caster sugar
30ml limoncello

In a saucepan, bring the milk and cream to the boil.

Mix the egg yolks and sugar in a bowl. Stir the hot liquid into the egg and sugar mix, and return to the saucepan. Place the saucepan over a low heat, and stir with a kitchen spoon until thickened. Strain through a fine sieve, add the limoncello and chill immediately.

To serve

mint leaves to garnish

Pour some anglaise in the middle of each serving plate. Place a chocolate marquise cup in the centre and top with a scoop of sherbet. Garnish with mint. In the photo the chef has placed a sugar hoop on top.

Serves 8

Recipe from Goran Zonai
SALSA BAR & GRILL
PORT DOUGLAS

Recommended wine:

De Bortoli Noble One
Botrytis Semillon 2003

Crisp Yellowfin Tuna Roulade

with lychee salad, pickled ginger and ponzu glaze

TUNA ROULADE

1 medium red capsicum, julienned
2 large carrots, peeled and julienned
2 spring onions, julienned
1 medium Japanese pickled cucumber, chopped
3 tablespoons QP mayonnaise (or regular mayonnaise, if Japanese mayo is not available)
salt and freshly ground black pepper
4 sheets nori
4 x 90g tuna strips
160g Katafi pastry
1 egg white
pinch of salt

Mix together all the vegetables with the mayonnaise and season to taste. Spread a quarter of the mixture on each nori sheet and place a tuna strip in the centre of each. Roll the sheets up tight, ensuring the tuna is centred.

Divide the pastry into four. Whisk the egg white with a pinch of salt, brush a little on the nori and quickly wrap each roulade in the pastry.

PICKLED GINGER AND PONZU GLAZE

120g grated dark palm sugar
40ml ponzu vinegar
40ml Champagne vinegar
40ml water
zest and juice of 1 lime
1/4 cup pickled ginger, sliced

Boil together all the ingredients until they reach a sticky, syrupy consistency. Strain through a fine sieve and cool until set.

To finish and serve

10 lychees
1 cup baby watercress

Sear the roulades on all sides in a hot frying pan with a little ghee until crisp. The tuna must remain rare.

Cut each roulade in half, then cut each half in two diagonally and stand in the centre of each serving plate. Drizzle with the glaze and garnish with lychees and watercress.

Serves 4

Recipe from Goran Zonai
SALSA BAR & GRILL
PORT DOUGLAS

Recommended wine:
Henschke Eleanor's Cottage Eden Valley Sauvignon Blanc/Semillon 2005

RIGHT: A cluster of fruit on one of the many varieties of palm to be found here.

ABOVE AND RIGHT: The Great Barrier Reef fascinates divers with its coral formations and tropical fish.

BELOW: Hand-blown glass vases by Chris Pantano capture the colours and life of the reef.

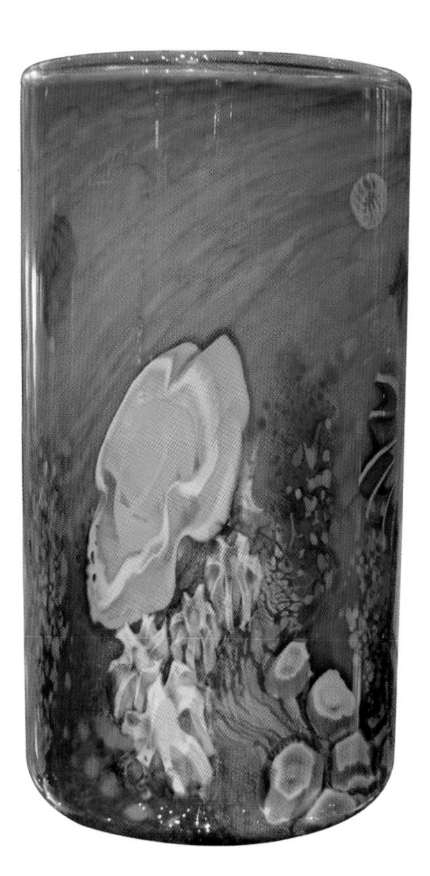

Veal and Roast Vegetable Stack

on blini with beetroot jus

2kg veal fillets
1kg red capsicums
1kg eggplants, sliced into rounds
1kg green zucchini, sliced lengthwise
500g sweet potatoes, well scrubbed
oil for roasting and frying

Preheat the oven to 175°C. Trim the veal fillets and cut into 120g portions. Bash flat with a meat mallet.

Roast the capsicums until blackened then peel, core and slice. To roast the eggplant and zucchini, brush a baking sheet lightly with oil. Put the eggplant and zucchini slices on the sheet and brush the tops lightly with oil. Bake for 20 minutes or until zucchini is lightly golden brown and just cooked through. Remove the zucchini, then turn the eggplants once and cook for another 20 minutes, until brown and soft.

Using a vegetable peeler, peel strips from the sweet potatoes. Shallow fry strips for 60 seconds, drain and set aside.

AVOCADO BLINI

600g plain flour
2 tablespoons baking powder
salt and freshly ground black pepper
750ml milk
3 eggs
1 cup chopped basil leaves
6 avocados, peeled and diced
300ml olive oil

Sift together the flour, baking powder, and salt and pepper. Add the milk and eggs and mix until smooth. Mix in the basil and avocado. Allow to rest for 30 minutes.

Heat the oil in a frying pan. Shallow-fry 8 equal portions of batter on both sides until golden and cooked through.

BEETROOT JUS

1 brown onion, peeled and diced
2 cloves garlic, peeled and crushed
oil for frying
500ml red wine
8 baby beetroot, peeled and diced
½ bunch thyme
2 litres beef stock
cornflour (if required)

Fry the onion and garlic in a little oil until browned. Add the red wine and bring to the boil. Simmer until reduced by half. Add the beetroot, thyme and beef stock, bring back to the boil and reduce by half. Strain into another saucepan, bring to the boil and thicken with cornflour if required.

To finish and serve

Pan-fry the veal fillets over medium heat for about 1 minute each side. Pour some Beetroot Jus in the centre of each serving plate. Place on top a blini, a portion of veal, an eggplant round, a zucchini strip and a capsicum slice. Top with the sweet potato chips.

Serves 8

Recipe from Bradley Andersen
MANGOSTIN'S RESTAURANT
CAIRNS

Recommended wine:
Bungawarra Shiraz 2005

BELOW: *Pink/blue Sealife Scent Bottle* in moulded glass by Tina Cooper.

LEFT: An acrylic on canvas painting, *Rainforest Journey,* by Heinz Steinmann.

ABOVE: In the tropical north the brightly coloured rainbow lorikeet competes for attention with vibrantly hued plants such as tropical ginger.

Roast Duck Breast

with spring onion rice cakes, master stock sauce and oyster mushrooms

4 duck breasts

Trim the fat back in line with the meat and score. Place skin-side up in the refrigerator overnight, uncovered, to air-dry (this creates a crisp skin).

SPRING ONION RICE CAKES

200g cooked rice (preferably slightly overcooked)
1 spring onion, finely sliced
1 egg
2 large cloves garlic, peeled and finely chopped
1 tablespoon finely chopped ginger
1 tablespoon finely chopped fresh coriander leaves
1 1/2 tablespoons sweet chilli sauce
salt to taste
cornflour

Mix all the ingredients well with enough cornflour to bind together. Form mixture into 4 patties, coat well with cornflour and set aside.

MASTER STOCK SAUCE

300ml beef or veal stock
1 small red chilli, split
3/4 cup bruised coriander stalks
2 star anise
80g caster sugar
150ml kecap manis
60ml rice vinegar
1 thumb ginger, peeled and sliced
cornflour

Simmer together all the ingredients in a saucepan until reduced by one-third, then strain and simmer again. Thicken to coating consistency with cornflour mixed with a little cold water. Set aside.

vegetable oil for frying
1 bunch asparagus, trimmed and halved
8 snow peas, sliced diagonally
8 oyster mushrooms, halved
30ml mirin
20ml Japanese soy sauce
1 small red chilli, deseeded and finely sliced
3cm thumb fresh ginger, julienned
100ml vegetable oil

Fry the rice cakes in oil in a non-stick frying pan. Drain on kitchen paper and keep warm.

Preheat the oven to 180°C. Bring a small saucepan of water to the boil for the vegetables.

Sear the flesh side of the duck breast in a hot baking pan, turn onto the fat side and place in the oven for 10 minutes.

Blanch the asparagus and snow peas in the boiling water for 2 minutes, then remove and combine with the mushrooms, mirin, soy sauce, chilli and ginger.

Reheat the master sauce.

To serve

Place a sliced duck breast on each rice cake, then stack the vegetables evenly on each serving. Drizzle with sauce.

NOTE: Make the Spring Onion Rice Cakes and the Master Stock Sauce the day before. The duck breast can also be prepared for air-drying the day before.

Serves 4

Recipe from Craig Squire
RED OCHRE GRILL
CAIRNS

Recommended wine:
Stella Bella Margaret River
Tempranillo 2004

RIGHT: Brilliant sprays of tropical honeysuckle are part of the vegetation of Northern Queensland.

Lamb Rack

with Lyonnaise potato, roast mushroom purée and mint sauce

LAMB AND SAUCE

1 tablespoon vegetable oil
4 x 4-rib lamb racks
125ml red wine
125ml beef stock
1 tablespoon mint sauce

Preheat the oven to 200°C. Heat the oil in a pan and sear the lamb until browned all over, then roast for 10 minutes. Remove from the oven, transfer to a tray and keep warm.

Pour the red wine into the pan and bring to the boil. Add the beef stock and simmer until reduced by half. Add the mint sauce and strain. Set aside and keep warm.

LYONNAISE POTATO

400g or about 10 small Kipfler potatoes, washed
1 brown onion, peeled and sliced
2 tablespoons olive oil
1 tablespoon butter

Place the potatoes in a saucepan of cold, salted water and bring to the boil. Reduce the heat and simmer for 20 minutes. Drain and slice 1cm thick. Sauté the onion in the olive oil until starting to colour. Add the potato and the butter and continue cooking until the potato begins to crisp.

ROAST MUSHROOM

200g button mushrooms
6 cloves garlic, peeled
6 sprigs thyme
2 tablespoons olive oil
½ teaspoon salt
¼ teaspoon freshly ground black pepper

Preheat the oven to 200°C. Place the mushrooms in a baking dish. Add the whole garlic cloves, thyme, olive oil, salt and pepper. Cover with tinfoil and roast for 20 minutes. Purée in a food processor.

To serve

Spoon some of the mushroom purée into the centre of each plate and arrange the potato and onion around the outside. Place a halved lamb rack on each portion of mushroom. Spoon the reserved mint sauce over and around the lamb.

Serves 4

Recipe from Ben Weatherhead
JAMES STREET BISTRO
BRISBANE

Recommended wine:
Cravers Heathcote Shiraz 2004

LEFT: Brisbane street sculptures in acrylic and steel.

ABOVE: This acrylic on canvas work by Marilyn Reeman is titled *Autumn to Winter.*

Grilled Moreton Bay Prawns

with lemon and rocket pesto and angel hair pasta

200g rocket
½ cup grated parmesan plus extra (shaved) to garnish
2 cloves garlic, peeled and crushed
½ cup toasted almond flakes plus extra
juice of 2 lemons
200–300ml olive oil
sea salt
cracked black pepper
200g angel hair pasta
800g green tiger prawns in the shell

Place the rocket, parmesan, garlic and almonds in a food processor and add the lemon juice. Blitz while adding olive oil until a wet paste forms. Season with sea salt and plenty of pepper. Set the pesto aside.

Cook the pasta in boiling water until al dente and set aside.

Remove the heads and shells from the prawns (leaving the tailpiece on for presentation) and devein. Fry in a little oil in a pan until just cooked. Add the rocket pesto and cooked pasta to the pan. Heat through then serve garnished with toasted almond flakes and shaved parmesan.

Serves 4 as an entrée

Recipe from Michael Wood
PIER NINE
BRISBANE

Recommended wine:
Sirromet Mount Cotton
Verdelho 2005

PIER

Crispy Skin Swains Reef King Snapper Fillets

with braised baby fennel and lemon garlic potatoes

BRAISED BABY FENNEL
8–12 baby fennel bulbs
juice of 1 lemon
pinch of salt
vegetable or chicken stock to cover
olive oil for frying
4 large golden shallots, peeled and coarsely chopped
4 cloves garlic, peeled and chopped
4 star anise
300ml dry white wine
1 litre chicken stock
100ml Pernod
300ml pouring cream
salt and freshly ground black pepper
squeeze of lemon juice
100g butter

Trim the stalks and base of the fennel bulbs, saving the trimmings for the sauce. Place the bulbs in a saucepan and squeeze lemon juice over. Add the salt and stock, cover with buttered paper and bring to a simmer. Cook gently for 8–10 minutes until tender. Remove from the saucepan. Increase the heat and reduce the liquid to 3–4 tablespoons.

Warm the olive oil in a frying pan. Add the fennel trimmings with the shallots, garlic and star anise. Cook without colouring over a medium heat for a few minutes. When softened, add the wine, bring to the boil and reduce to three-quarters. Add the chicken stock and simmer until reduced by half. Add the Pernod and cream, and return to a simmer. Season with salt and pepper and a squeeze of lemon juice. Strain, squeezing the juice out of the fennel trimmings. Whisk in the butter.

LEMON GARLIC POTATOES
4 large King Edward potatoes
olive oil for frying and rubbing
salt
1 teaspoon cayenne pepper
2 cloves garlic, peeled and crushed
100g butter
grated zest and juice of 1 lemon
4 x 200g king snapper fillets, skin on
freshly ground black pepper

Boil the potatoes in their skins. Allow to cool (so they won't crumble), then peel with the back of a knife. Cut into 2cm cubes.

In a frying pan, colour the potatoes evenly in a little olive oil over a medium heat. Season with salt and cayenne pepper. Add the garlic, butter and lemon zest and juice.

Preheat the oven to 200°C. Heat a heavy-based frying pan over a moderate heat. Rub the skin of the snapper with olive oil, and season with salt and pepper. Fry skin-side down for 2 minutes then place in the hot oven for 4 minutes (skin-side down). Remove from the oven, turn and allow to rest for a few minutes.

To serve
Place some potatoes in the centre of each plate and top with a snapper fillet, then 2–3 fennel bulbs and drizzle with the fennel sauce.

Serves 4

Recipe from Michael Wood
PIER NINE
BRISBANE

Recommended wine:
Sirromet Mount Cotton
Cabernet Sauvignon
Merlot 2003

Cabbage, Bacon and Raisin-filled Chicken Breast

with twice-baked morel mushroom soufflé and tarragon jus

MOREL MUSHROOM SOUFFLÉ

20g soft butter
50g breadcrumbs
50g (about 13) dried morels, ground into powder
100g butter
100g flour
300ml milk
4 egg yolks
12 egg whites

Preheat the oven to 180°C. Butter 10 medium-sized ramekins with the soft butter and place in the fridge. Mix together the breadcrumbs and 10g of the morel powder and coat the inside of the ramekins with this.

Heat a pan gently, add the butter and melt. Stir in the flour and cook for 5 minutes to make a roux (do not allow to colour). Gradually add the milk, stirring continuously until smooth. Stir in the remaining morel powder and the egg yolks. Transfer the mixture to a clean bowl.

Beat the egg whites to peaks, fold half into the roux, then gently fold in the remaining whites. Place the mixture in the ramekins.

Put the ramekins in a deep ovenproof dish, filled halfway with hot water and place in the oven for 30 minutes. Do not open the oven during cooking. Take the ramekins out of the water and set aside to cool.

FILLED CHICKEN BREASTS

10 single organic or corn-fed chicken breasts, skin on
3 cups finely chopped Savoy cabbage
1/3 cup raisins
6 rashers middle bacon, rind removed
oil for frying
salt and freshly ground black pepper
75ml white wine
350ml chicken jus or stock
1 teaspoon chopped fresh tarragon

Make an incision in the side of each chicken breast to form a pocket.

Blanch and refresh the cabbage and raisins. Cut the bacon into lardons and fry in a little oil until golden. Add the cabbage and raisins to the pan, season and cook. Cool.

Preheat the oven to 200°C. Stuff the chicken breasts with the cabbage mixture.

Heat a frying pan with a little oil, brown the breasts skin-side first, then turn over to seal the base. Place on an oven tray and bake for 15–20 minutes. Set aside to rest.

In a pan simmer the wine until reduced by half, add the jus and the tarragon and simmer for 30 seconds.

To serve

Remove the soufflés from the ramekins by running a knife around the edges and shaking them out. Place the soufflés on a tray in the oven at 200°C for 5 minutes, then add the chicken to reheat for 5 minutes.

Place a soufflé on one side of each serving plate, a halved chicken breast on an angle on the other and drizzle jus in the centre.

Serves 10

Recipe from Andrew Budgen
ERA BISTRO
SOUTH BRISBANE

Recommended wine:

Kaesler Stonehorse Grenache/Shiraz/Mourvedre 2005

LEFT ABOVE: By Gillian Buttress-Grove, *Dunegrass II*, is a painting using high gloss enamel on board.

LEFT: Grass trees and kangaroo paws are some of the native flora found in Roma Street Parklands in the heart of Brisbane.

RIGHT: *Mermaids* by Stephen McLean, also known as Duk Duk, is an acrylic on parchment painting that reflects the artist's unique style and his affinity with traditional aboriginal art.

Glazed Lemon Tart

with clotted cream ice cream and passionfruit purée

GLAZED LEMON TART

250g sugar
grated zest and juice of 4 lemons
500ml cream
9 eggs
1 x 28cm sweet tart shell

Preheat the oven to 100°C. Bring the sugar, and lemon zest and juice to the boil, then set aside.

Bring the cream to the boil separately, then set aside. In a bowl, beat the eggs, pour in the lemon mixture, then the cream and mix well. Pass through a sieve into a double boiler and cook the custard, stirring, until thick. Pour into the tart shell and bake at 180°c for about 35 minutes until cooked.

Tap the oven tray and if there is no wobble in the tart filling, it is ready. Remove from the oven, leave to cool, then refrigerate.

CLOTTED CREAM ICE CREAM

5 egg yolks
100g sugar
250ml milk
250ml clotted cream

Mix the egg yolks in a bowl with the sugar. Bring the milk and clotted cream to the boil, then pour slowly into the egg mix, stirring continuously. Return to the saucepan and heat gently, stirring, until the mixture covers the back of a spoon. Pass through a fine sieve and cool.

Precool the ice cream machine, pour in the mixture and mix until smooth and creamy. Remove and freeze.

To serve
10 passionfruit
sugar for topping

Halve the passionfruit, scoop out the pulp and place in a bowl. Reserve the shells.

Cut the tart into 10 pieces, sprinkle with a little sugar and glaze with a blowtorch until caramelised. Place a slice on each plate with some of the pulp and a scoop of ice cream in a passionfruit shell.

Serves 10

Recipe from Andrew Budgen
ERA BISTRO
SOUTH BRISBANE

Recommended wine:
Wellington Iced Riesling 2005

Caramelised Pork Belly

with scampi, gai lan, fried lotus root and sticky plum sauce

STICKY PLUM SAUCE

1 x 850g can plums
2 star anise
8 cardamom pods
250ml Chinese rice cooking wine
2cm thumb ginger
800g sugar
1 medium onion, peeled and sliced
2 tablespoons finely sliced lemongrass
4 cloves garlic, peeled
40g tamarind pulp
375ml rice vinegar

Make the sauce first as you will use it for the marinade as well as a garnish. Place all the ingredients in a saucepan and bring to the boil. Reduce to a medium heat and simmer for 25 minutes. Turn off the heat and allow the flavours to infuse for at least 10 minutes. Strain through a sieve and set aside.

PORK

1kg pork belly, skinned and deboned
400g whole, peeled scampi
oil for frying
salt and freshly ground black pepper
1 bunch gai lan (available from Asian food stores)
1 tablespoon butter
8 slices lotus root (available from Asian food stores)

Preheat the oven to 180°C. Take 1 cup of the reserved sauce for basting. Place the pork on a roasting rack in a baking dish, brush with the sauce and place in the oven. Cook for about 1½ hours, depending on the thickness of the meat, basting every 20 minutes with more of the sauce.

Remove the meat from the oven and allow to cool for 20 minutes. When cool and firm, slice into 8 strips. Place under a grill and reheat.

Fry the scampi in a little oil for 3–4 minutes. Meanwhile plunge the gai lan into boiling, salted water for 30 seconds. Drain. Toss the butter through the scampi and season. Remove from the pan and keep warm.

Add a little more oil to the pan and fry the lotus root until golden.

To serve

Divide the gai lan among serving plates. Top with scampi, then pork and lotus root. Drizzle some of the reserved plum sauce around and serve immediately.

NOTE: The remaining plum sauce will keep in the refrigerator for at least 1 month and can be used as a dipping sauce.

Serves 4

Recipe from Kate Harvey
HARVEY'S RESTAURANT
BRISBANE

Recommended wine:
Cascabel Fleurieu
McLaren Vale Shiraz 2003

Bitter Chocolate Mousse

with mascarpone custard and cherry sauce

BITTER CHOCOLATE MOUSSE

300g dark chocolate
60g butter
3 teaspoons espresso coffee
½ nip Galliano
½ nip Kirsch
7 eggs, separated
60g (about 6 tablespoons) sugar

Place the chocolate and butter in a saucepan over a bain-marie, stirring. Once the chocolate has melted add the coffee and alcohol. Whisk in the egg yolks, 1 at a time. Remove from the heat and allow to cool slightly. Beat the egg whites with the sugar to soft peaks, then fold gently into the chocolate mix.

MASCARPONE CUSTARD

5 egg yolks
100g sugar
500g mascarpone
4 egg whites

Whisk the egg yolks, sugar and mascarpone until thick and pale. Whisk the egg whites to soft peaks and carefully fold into the mascarpone mix.

CHERRY SAUCE

500ml sugar syrup (heat 500g sugar and 500ml water until sugar has dissolved)
1 cinnamon quill
1 vanilla bean
1 star anise
300ml cherry brandy
100ml brandy
1kg fresh cherries, stones and stems removed

Place all the ingredients except the cherries in a saucepan and bring to the boil. Simmer for 30–40 minutes or until the syrup has reduced by a third. Add the cherries and simmer for another 15 minutes, stirring occasionally. Remove from the heat and allow to cool.

To serve

Divide the cherries and syrup between 6 parfait glasses. Spoon in layers of the mousse and the custard alternately. Finish with another spoonful of cherries and syrup.

NOTE: For the photograph, the chef has spooned cherry sauce on to the plate and served the custard and mousse in elegant chocolate moulds.

Serves 6

Recipe from Kristie Rickman
HARVEY'S RESTAURANT
BRISBANE

Recommended wine:
Rutherglen Estate Muscat 2004

LEFT: *Angel Unaware* was carved by Peter Chapman from a black wattle trunk.

Tian of Sand Crab and Avocado

with blini, cured salmon and avruga caviar

DRESSING

30ml (6 teaspoons) fresh lemon juice
1 teaspoon Dijon mustard
100ml good quality olive oil
pinch of salt and cracked pepper

Mix the lemon juice and mustard in a bowl. Slowly whisk in the olive oil. Season with salt and pepper.

BLINI

5g fresh yeast or 1/2 teaspoon dry yeast
80g plain flour
1/4 cup milk
1 egg yolk
1/4 cup warm milk
1 egg white
2 tablespoons cream, whipped
oil for frying

Mix together the yeast, 20g of the flour and all the milk, and leave to rise for 20 minutes in a warm place. Mix the egg yolk, warm milk and the remaining 60g of flour and add to the yeast mixture. Beat the egg white and add to the batter along with the whipped cream. Allow the batter to rest for 30 minutes, then fry spoonfuls of mixture to make small round pancakes. Serve immediately.

TIAN

200g fresh sand crab meat
1 tablespoon crème fraîche or sour cream
flaky salt and freshly cracked pepper
2 ripe avocados, peeled and diced
1 teaspoon lemon juice
1 teaspoon good quality olive oil

Mix the crab and crème fraîche with a pinch of salt and pepper. Combine the avocado, lemon juice, olive oil, salt and pepper. Using a ring mould, shape a quarter of the avocado into a mound in the centre of each plate, place a quarter of the crab mix on top of each, then remove the mould.

To finish and serve

80g smoked salmon
microgreens to garnish
50g avruga caviar (or golden herring roe can be substituted)
crème fraîche to garnish

Arrange a quarter of the salmon on top of each tian and garnish with microgreens and dressing. Arrange the blini, caviar and crème fraîche to one side.

NOTE: Savoury pancakes or fresh sliced bread can be substituted for the blini.

Serves 4

Recipe from Joshua Philippi
JOSEPH'S FINE DINING & SUPPER
BRISBANE

Recommended wine:

Paradigm Hill Mornington Peninsula
Pinot Noir Rosé 2004

BELOW: An oil on canvas work by Ken Farrow entitled *Noosa National Park.*

LEFT: *Driftwood* is a large mixed media work by artist and designer Tony Grainger.

Seared Queensland Scallops

with angel hair pasta and smoked-tomato beurre blanc

BEURRE BLANC

100g smoked tomatoes
100g semi-dried tomatoes
1 teaspoon smoked paprika
200ml vegetable oil
1 stick lemongrass, chopped
1 sprig thyme, chopped
2 golden shallots, peeled and chopped
¼ fennel bulb, chopped
150g cold butter, diced
100ml white wine
100ml fish stock
1 tablespoon white wine vinegar
50ml cream
juice of ½ lemon
salt and freshly ground black pepper

Put the first 4 ingredients in a blender and process to a fine purée. Pour into fine muslin and let hang for at least 1 hour, saving the drained oil. Set aside.

Sweat the lemongrass, thyme, shallots and fennel in a little of the butter then add the wine, stock and vinegar, and simmer until reduced by two-thirds. Add the cream and bring to the boil. Add the rest of the cold butter a little at a time while constantly whisking. Mix in 2 tablespoons of the smoked tomato purée. Season with the lemon juice, and salt and pepper. Pass the sauce through a fine strainer and set aside, keeping warm.

To finish and serve

1 Roma tomato, diced
50g semi-dried tomatoes, diced
25g smoked tomatoes, diced
angel hair pasta (see 'Recipes Continued' on page 190)
24 Hervey Bay scallops, roe removed
chopped chives to garnish

Make a salsa by mixing all three kinds of the tomatoes with the oil reserved from the purée.

Cook the pasta in boiling, salted water then drain.

Meanwhile, sear the scallops in a hot pan on one side for 20–25 seconds. Turn over and seal quickly (for medium-rare). Remove from the pan.

Arrange a portion of pasta in the centre of each plate and surround with 6 scallops. Drizzle with the beurre blanc and scatter with the salsa and chives.

Serves 4

Recipe from Daran Glasgow
CHILL ON TEDDER
DINING AND WINE BAR
MAIN BEACH

Recommended wine:

Symphony Hill Wines Reserve
Granite Belt Verdelho 2005

Tempura Crab

with cucumber and tomato salad

CRAB

2 soft-shell crabs, cleaned
salt and freshly ground black pepper
100g tempura flour (available from Asian food stores)
1/4 cup ice-cold water
oil for deep-frying
1 tablespoon basil mayonnaise (add fresh chopped basil to mayonnaise)

Dry the crabs with kitchen paper. Sprinkle with salt and pepper. Mix the tempura flour with the iced water until you have a smooth consistency. Cut each crab in half and lightly coat with the tempura batter.

Deep-fry at 190°C for 2–3 minutes or until browned.

CUCUMBER AND TOMATO SALAD

1/2 cucumber
1/2 avocado, peeled
1 tomato, deseeded
1/4 cup mint leaves
1/4 cup flat-leaf parsley leaves
1 tablespoon olive oil
2 tablespoons Chardonnay vinaigrette (available from good food stores)

Julienne the cucumber, avocado and tomato. Mix with the mint and parsley leaves. Drizzle the olive oil, then the Chardonnay vinaigrette over the salad mixture and toss.

To serve

Divide the salad between 2 plates. Arrange the fried crab pieces on top. Drizzle the basil mayonnaise over the crab and serve.

Serves 2

Recipe from Philip J. Murphy
BUTTER BISTRO
BRISBANE

Recommended wine:
Groom Adelaide Hills
Sauvignon Blanc 2005

BELOW: Yachts at Kangaroo Point Marina on the Brisbane River.

Tomato Confit in Vanilla Oil

with eggplant ice cream

EGGPLANT ICE CREAM

½ large eggplant
1 clove garlic, peeled and chopped
3 tablespoons salt-reduced soy sauce

Preheat the oven to 150°C. Peel the eggplant and sprinkle with the garlic and soy sauce. Wrap in tinfoil and bake in the oven for 30 minutes. While hot, purée in a food processor, then freeze for 2 hours.

TOMATO CONFIT

12 vine-ripened tomatoes
4 cloves garlic, peeled and finely sliced
150ml olive oil
1 vanilla bean
2 spring onions, thinly sliced

Blanch the tomatoes in boiling water, cut in half and deseed, then place in a single layer in a deep tray.

Infuse the garlic in the olive oil for 30 minutes with the scraped vanilla bean. Preheat the oven to 130°C. Pour the strained oil over the tomatoes, cover with tinfoil and bake in the oven for 35 minutes.

Cool the tomatoes, then place in 4 round or square 6–7cm moulds in alternate layers with the spring onion. Set them aside.

To serve

fresh chervil to garnish

Place a mould of confit in the centre of each plate, remove the mould, top with a scoop of ice cream and garnish with fresh chervil.

Serves 4

Recipe from Meyjitte Boughenout
ABSYNTHE RESTAURANT
SURFERS PARADISE

Recommended wine:
Domaine A 'Lady A' Coal River Valley
Fumé Blanc 2003

RIGHT: This sculpture by Mark Warne called *Reef Fetish* uses rust, ceramic, shell and fish hooks.

Where heritage comes alive

Northern Territory

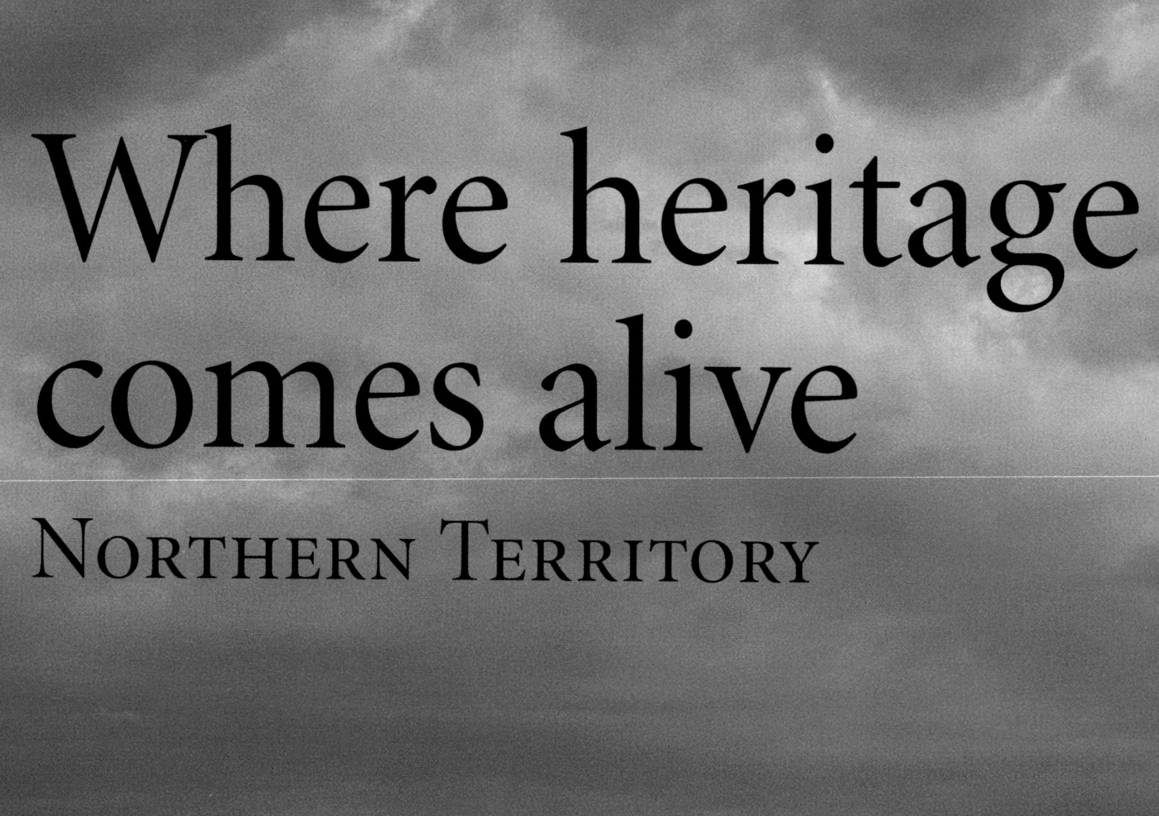

SPECTACULAR – THAT IS THE WORD that best sums up the Northern Territory. Equivalent in size to France, Italy and Spain combined, this sprawling region contains within its boundaries two World Heritage parks – Kakadu and Uluru-Kata Tjuta, usually called simply Uluru, and better known internationally as Ayers Rock.

With Aboriginal people making up one-third of the state's population, there is a major emphasis on indigenous art and cultural pursuits dating back to times long before the arrival of the first European settlers. Several organisations offer 'walkabout' tours of Uluru and other attractions, and local guides introduce visitors to practices and sights that they would never discover on their own.

Bush tucker feasts include witchetty grubs, roasted lizards and other traditional delicacies, and are likely to be followed by dances and songs passed down through many generations.

Aboriginal art, much of which is highly regarded, is well represented at a number of galleries throughout the region. And should you visit any of them, there is a good chance that you will meet an artist or two, happy to discuss their work.

In the city of Darwin, cafés and restaurants make good use of local ingredients. With the ocean on three sides of its peninsula setting, there is a major emphasis on seafood, and the year-round warm climate makes outdoor dining highly desirable and almost always possible. The Wharf Precinct offers wall-to-wall eateries, all with a view over the adjacent marina and out to sea.

Colourful stalls at the city's many weekly markets emphasise the fact that more than 50 nationalities are represented in the Territory's population of 100 000 inhabitants.

The Northern Territory climate is far from ideal for grape-growing, but that hasn't stopped Chateau Hornsby, established at Alice Springs in the 1970s, from gaining a far-reaching reputation. Nearly all of its production is sold at the cellar door, but enthusiasts visiting the property's restaurant and tourist facilities invariably buy a bottle or two to take home to share with friends.

LEFT: The Stuart Highway, approximately 2,800km long, connects Adelaide in South Australia to Darwin in the Northern Territory.

ABOVE: *Emu in Landscape* is an acrylic on canvas work by Heinz Steinmann.

Timbale of Port Parham Crab

1kg sweet carrots, julienned
1kg white radishes, julienned
softened butter for greasing moulds
2 x 1kg fresh cooked crabs
finely grated zest and juice of 1 lemon
50ml thick cream
4 sprigs dill, finely chopped
4 sprigs chives, finely chopped
150g softened butter
2 punnets cherry tomatoes, each cut into 4–6 wedges
4 sprigs curly parsley
4 small inner stalks celery, leafy tips only

Cook the carrots and radishes in boiling, salted water until tender, then drain and refrigerate until chilled.

Butter the insides of four 6cm-high plastic ring moulds. Alternating the carrots and radishes, press them upright around the inside of the rings, then refrigerate.

When the rings are set, with a sharp knife trim the tops of the carrots and radishes level with the top of the rings.

Remove the flesh from the crabs, picking out any bits of shell. Place the crab meat in a chilled mixing bowl, add the lemon zest and mix well with a wooden spoon. Mix in the lemon juice, then the cream, forming a smooth paste. Gently mix in the chopped dill and chives, then add the softened butter and incorporate well.

Spoon the mixture into the plastic rings, packing in well until level with tops of the carrots and radishes. Smooth off with a palette knife and refrigerate to set.

To serve

Remove the timbales from the plastic moulds and place on plates. Place a celery curl and a sprig of parsley on each timbale and garnish with the cherry tomato wedges. Serve chilled.

Serves 4

Recipe from Neill Sharer
KUNIYA RESTAURANT,
SAILS IN THE DESERT HOTEL
AYERS ROCK (ULURU)

Recommended wine:

Chalice Bridge Estate Margaret River Semillon/Sauvignon Blanc 2005

ABOVE: On the Stuart Highway in Australia's central desert between Alice Springs and Darwin are the Devil's Marbles, a group of large boulders seemingly precariously balanced.

RIGHT: *Tribal Gathering* by Rindy is an acrylic on board painting.

White Chocolate and Orange Cheesecake

with strawberry dust, ginger shortbread and vanilla fig jam

VANILLA FIG JAM

½ vanilla bean
200g fresh figs, halved
100g caster sugar
2 star anise
½ cinnamon stick

Split the vanilla bean and scrape the seeds into a saucepan. Add the rest of the ingredients and mix to coat in sugar. Place on a high heat and stir continuously until mixture is lightly caramelised. Refrigerate for 24 hours.

ORANGE CHEESECAKE

500g Callebaut white chocolate
5 egg yolks
zest of 1 orange
100g caster sugar
500g cream cheese, softened
100g mascarpone

Melt the chocolate in a microwave on high in 15-second bursts. Whisk the egg yolks, zest and sugar until pale and thick. In a food processor mix the cream cheese and mascarpone until smooth, add the chocolate then lightly fold in the egg mixture. Refrigerate for 24 hours.

GINGER SHORTBREAD

300g butter
1 tablespoon minced ginger
1 egg plus 1 egg yolk
300g caster sugar
350g plain flour

Melt the butter with the ginger in a small saucepan.

Beat the egg and the egg yolk and sugar until pale and thick, then drizzle in the butter and ginger mixture, whisking to combine. Sift the flour and fold into the egg mixture. Spoon into a 1cm-deep 25 x 15cm lined baking tray and refrigerate for 1 hour.

Bake at 160°C for 30 minutes. Allow to cool, then cut out four 5cm-diameter rounds using a cookie cutter.

STRAWBERRY DUST

200g fresh strawberries
50g caster sugar

Hull the strawberries and slice very thinly. Place on a tray lined with baking paper. Bake at 80°C until crisp (about 4 hours).

In a small food processor pulse the strawberry crisps with the sugar until finely ground.

TOFFEE HALO

200g caster sugar
50ml corn syrup
1 teaspoon water

Place all the ingredients in a saucepan and boil until a very light golden colour. Using a fork, swirl the toffee onto greased baking paper to make halo shapes.

To serve

mint sprigs
fresh strawberries

Using an ice cream scoop, make balls of cheesecake. Roll each in the strawberry dust. Place a shortbread disc in the centre of each plate with a cheesecake ball on top. Top with a toffee halo and dot vanilla fig jam around the plate. Garnish with mint and fresh strawberries.

Serves 4

Recipe from Simon Matthews
PEE WEE'S AT THE POINT
DARWIN

Recommended wine:
Ballandean Estate Granite Belt
Late Harvest Sylvaner 2000

ABOVE AND RIGHT: Uluru, also known as Ayers Rock, is a large sandstone formation sacred to the Aboriginal people of the area. Caves in the rock have been decorated with paintings and prehistoric art up to 10,000 years old and may indicate such things as the whereabouts of water and other vital information.

Salt and Szechuan Soft-shell Crab

with crisp chilli bean shoot salad

FLOUR MIX

50g Szechuan pepper
20g Chinese five spice powder
50g Maldon sea salt
20g whole black peppercorns
500g rice flour

Dry-fry the Szechuan pepper in a small pan until fragrant, then pound with a mortar and pestle until coarsely ground. Mix with the rest of the ingredients. Set aside.

DRESSING

200ml Thai fish sauce
200ml rice wine vinegar
200g dark palm sugar
50g red Thai curry paste

Place all the ingredients in a small saucepan and simmer to reduce by half, stirring continuously to ensure the sugar dissolves. Chill.

SALAD

3 long red chillies
vegetable oil for frying
100g bean shoots
1/3 cup coriander leaves
1/3 cup Thai basil leaves
1 small red onion, peeled and finely sliced
2 tablespoons fried shallots (available from Asian food stores)

Slice the chillies lengthwise into matchsticks, removing the seeds. Add 2cm of oil to a hot wok and fry the chillies until crisp, then drain on kitchen paper. Toss all the ingredients together with the dressing.

To finish and serve

2 litres cottonseed oil
8 x 150g soft-shell crabs, carapace and gills removed
kecap manis
Thai basil leaves
fried shallots

Heat the oil in a wok to 180°C. Toss the crabs in the flour mix, shake off excess then drop into the wok. Fry for 1 minute, then drain on kitchen paper.

On each of 4 plates, layer the salad and 2 crabs into a 10cm presentation ring. Drizzle kecap manis around the edge of each plate. Top the stacks with basil leaves and fried shallots. Remove the rings to serve.

Serves 4

Recipe from Simon Matthews
PEE WEE'S AT THE POINT
DARWIN

Recommended wine:
Pikes Clare Valley 2005 Riesling

BELOW: Sun and dust silhouette outback drovers at work.

Crisp-skin Mirin-cured Barramundi

with green papaya rice paper rolls

MIRIN-CURED BARRAMUNDI

1kg barramundi fillet, skin on
200ml mirin
1 tablespoon Maldon sea salt
1 tablespoon caster sugar
zest of 2 limes

Soak the fillet skin-side down in mirin for 10 minutes, then drain. Mix together the remaining ingredients and spread over the fillet. Cover and refrigerate for 24 hours.

Scrape off the curing mixture, roll the fillet lengthwise in plastic cling film very firmly and refrigerate for another 24 hours.

GREEN PAPAYA RICE PAPER ROLLS

½ green papaya, peeled, deseeded and julienned
10 cherry tomatoes, quartered
⅓ cup mint leaves
⅓ cup coriander leaves
1 long red chilli, deseeded and chopped
50g grated palm sugar
3 tablespoons lime juice
2 tablespoons fish sauce
16 x 16cm rice paper wrappers

Toss together all the filling ingredients and allow to stand for 1 hour. Fill a bowl with hot water and soak the rice paper wrappers, one at a time, for 10 seconds until soft. Lay out on a bench greased with sesame oil, place some papaya mix across the centre of the paper, fold the wrapper over the mixture, fold the sides in and roll as tightly as possible. Repeat with the rest of wrappers, keeping the finished rolls under a damp cloth.

CHILLI RELISH

30g dried shrimps
30 dried long chillies
cottonseed oil for deep-frying
10 cloves garlic, peeled and chopped
12 red shallots, peeled and chopped
100ml fish sauce
100g grated palm sugar
2 tablespoons tamarind paste

Soak the dried shrimps in hot water for 15 minutes, then drain and dry well. Soak the dried chillies in hot water for 2 minutes, then drain and dry well. Remove the stems, deseed and chop.

Heat the oil in a hot wok to 180°C. Deep-fry the shrimps, chilli, garlic and shallots in small batches until golden, then drain on kitchen paper. Process all the fried ingredients in a small food processor, then transfer back to a hot, dry wok and add the remaining ingredients. Simmer, stirring, until thick.

To finish and serve

oil for frying
1 bunch bok choy, steamed
dipping sauce (see 'Recipes Continued' on page 190)

2 limes, halved
Thai basil leaves

Trim the tail end off the barramundi and cut the roll into 4 portions. Sear on all sides in a hot pan in oil until the skin crisps and the fish is warmed through.

Stack 4 papaya rolls on each of 4 serving plates in a criss-cross fashion, top with some bok choy, then place a barramundi portion on top.

Put a dish of dipping sauce on each plate and a spoonful of chilli relish on the barramundi. Garnish with a lime half and some Thai basil.

Serves 4

Recipe from Simon Matthews
PEE WEE'S AT THE POINT
DARWIN

Recommended wine:

Cockfighter's Ghost Langhorne Creek
Cabernet Sauvignon 2005

IT'S BIG, IT'S BOLD and it's far enough from other population centres to have developed a distinct character of its own. Those are just three of the many reasons that Western Australia is a fascinating place to visit.

This sprawling region has history on its side. It was founded in 1829, five years before Victoria and seven years before South Australia.

Its first grape vines were planted in the same year. Local wine was being sold in good quantities by 1842, several years before the same could be said for states on the other side of the country.

Those early wines came from the Swan Valley, still home to many quality-oriented producers, but in recent years Margaret River and the Lower Great Southern region have gained equal status.

As happens elsewhere, the establishment of a thriving local wine industry has spawned a love of good food. Perth boasts an impressive number of cafés and restaurants, and travellers will have no trouble finding gustatory satisfaction in outlying areas.

Local chefs delight in using local ingredients in their dishes, and the state's geographic isolation has spawned a style that has some interesting points of difference from those on the eastern and southern coasts.

Visitors can even travel while they taste, courtesy of the 'Spirit of the West' dining train.

The state has a thriving art community, and as is the case in other parts of the country, many local artists take their inspiration from the colours of nature around them.

Western Australia has great beaches and abundant wildlife, some of which can be seen at close quarters in the renowned Perth Zoo.

One of the more unusual local attractions in the state is Whale World, which gives visitors a view of a very different time in Australian history, when whale hunting was seen solely as a highly profitable industry.

LEFT: Perth, commonly referred to by tourists as 'the friendly city', provides a wonderful variety of evening meals complemented by local wines.

LEFT: This oil on board painting by Len Zuks, *Johnston St. Trees,* captures some of the atmosphere of the artist's home town of Boddington.

Duck Bastillas

sunflower oil
3kg duck Maryland
12 medium brown onions, peeled and chopped
12 cloves garlic, peeled and chopped
1 teaspoon saffron threads
2 tablespoons ground cinnamon
1 tablespoon ground cumin
2 tablespoons ground turmeric
chilli to taste
¼ cup sherry, or to taste
9 litres chicken stock
6 large eggs at room temperature
salt and freshly ground black pepper
⅔ cup chopped fresh parsley
1 cup chopped fresh coriander
12 sheets filo pastry
¼ cup melted butter
100g flaked almonds, toasted
ground cinnamon to garnish

Heat some oil in a heavy pan and sauté the duck pieces until golden brown. Add the next 8 ingredients, adding more oil if necessary. Stir to coat the duck well.

Add the sherry and stock, bring to the boil, then lower the heat and simmer for 45–50 minutes until the duck is tender. Set aside to cool.

Remove the meat (reserve the liquid), discarding the skin and bones, and shred finely.

Reduce the poaching liquid by half and remove from the heat. Add the eggs and whisk until well combined. Pour this mixture into a small saucepan, season and scramble over a gentle heat until creamy and nearly set. Stir in the parsley and coriander, and check the seasoning. Allow the mixture to cool completely. Stir the meat into the egg mixture, taste for seasoning and refrigerate until ready to use.

To make the pies, work with 1 sheet of pastry at a time. Place 2 sheets on the work surface and brush each with melted butter. Fold each in half then cut into 6 equal squares. Put these to one side (you will need only 10).

Place the remaining 10 filo sheets on the work surface and brush with melted butter. Fold each in half and brush with butter. Fold in half again.

Preheat the oven to 200°C. Place a generous tablespoon of the meat mixture in the centre of each filo square. Place one of the small pastry squares on top of the filling and scatter a teaspoon of toasted almonds over the top. Brush around the filling with melted butter then bring the surrounding pastry sides up and over the filling to form a ball. Turn the pie over and, with the palms of your hands, gently shape into a raised circular pie. Flatten the top slightly and refrigerate until ready to bake.

Place the pies on a greased oven tray and bake for 10–15 minutes until golden brown.

Remove the pies and sprinkle with cinnamon to serve.

Makes 10

Recipe from Brad Leahy
BLUE WATER GRILL
PERTH

Recommended wine:
Wignalls Albany Pinot Noir 2005

Hot Chocolate Filo Pudding

with cherries in port and crème fraîche

CHOCOLATE LAVA FILLING

85g Callebaut dark chocolate
80g unsalted butter
2 egg yolks
2 whole eggs
50g caster sugar
25g plain flour

Melt the chocolate and butter in a pan over a bain-marie. Meanwhile, whisk the egg yolks, eggs and sugar until very pale. Once at the 'ribbon' stage (about 3 minutes from start to finish when using a whisk), fold through the melted chocolate. Carefully sift the flour and fold through the mix. Refrigerate until set.

CHERRIES IN PORT

100g dried Morello cherries
400ml port
1 vanilla bean
1 teaspoon cornflour

Place the cherries, port and vanilla bean in a small saucepan and carefully simmer until there is just enough liquid to cover the cherries. Mix the cornflour with a little water and add to thicken the cherry mixture. Refrigerate until serving time.

To finish and serve

8 sheets filo pastry
¼ cup clarified butter
crème fraîche to serve
icing sugar for dusting

Take 1 sheet of filo pastry at a time and fold into 4, brushing clarified butter between each layer. Place 2 tablespoons of the chocolate filling in the centre and bring up the sides to make the shape of a bonbon. Make 8. Place each parcel in a metal ramekin and refrigerate for 1 hour.

Preheat the oven to 200°C. Bake the puddings for 10–11 minutes. Remove from the oven and place a pudding in the centre of each plate and spoon the cherry mix around.

Top with a large dollop of crème fraîche and dust with icing sugar. The centres should ooze warm chocolate.

Serves 8

Recipe from Brad Leahy
BLUE WATER GRILL
PERTH

Recommended wine:
Woody Nook Nooky Delight

LEFT: Estimated to be 3000 million years old, the awesome 25-metre-high granite Wave Rock at Hyden has been sculpted by nature.

ABOVE: One of a series of billboards celebrating the various immigrant communities of Western Australia, this was created by a number of local Greek artists.

Seared Scallops

with dukka, sesame dressing and salad

SESAME DRESSING

500g dark miso paste
500g tahini
500ml rice vinegar
2 tablespoons sesame oil
2 tablespoons ginger oil
4 tablespoons sugar
100ml mirin
2 tablespoons wasabi powder
400ml water

Blend together all the ingredients. Set aside.

DUKKA

1 cup sesame seeds
1/2 cup hazelnuts
3/4 cup coriander seeds
4 tablespoons cumin seeds
1 teaspoon salt
1/2 teaspoon black peppercorns
1 teaspoon dried thyme or mint

Separately dry-toast the seeds and nuts until lightly coloured. Remove the skins from the hazelnuts. When cooled pound all the ingredients into a coarse powder.

SEARED SCALLOPS

24 Western Australian scallops
1 handful curly endive salad, washed and dried
1 handful watercress, picked over
1 bunch chervil, picked over
6 tomatoes, halved and lightly baked
2 red onions, peeled and julienned
70ml Australian verjuice
70ml extra virgin olive oil
sea salt to taste
2 chillies, chopped

Clean the scallops and remove the muscle. Mix together the endive, watercress, chervil, tomatoes and onions. Sear the scallops on a flat grill. Mix the verjuice and olive oil and toss through the salad.

To serve

Spoon the sesame dressing on to each plate followed by 4 scallops. Sprinkle the dukka on the scallops until it sticks, then top with the salad. Spoon around extra dressing and sprinkle some chillies over.

Serves 6

Recipe from Chris Taylor
FRASER'S RESTAURANT
PERTH

Recommended wine:

Plantagenet Mt Barker
Great Southern Riesling 2005

Pearl Barley and Porcini Risotto

with pink snapper

PEARL BARLEY AND PORCINI RISOTTO

oil for frying
1 clove garlic, peeled and minced
1 medium onion, peeled and finely diced
80g dried porcini mushrooms, soaked then diced
1 cup pearl barley, blanched then refreshed
1.5 litres chicken stock
30g parmesan, grated
50g butter, diced
½ bunch English spinach, blanched then chopped
salt and freshly ground black pepper

6 x 160g pink snapper fillets, skin on, scaled

Heat a little oil in a pan and sauté the garlic and onion without colouring. Add the porcini and sauté. Add the barley and 1 cup of stock and cook, stirring, until the liquid is absorbed. Continue adding stock a little at a time until all is absorbed. This should take 10–12 minutes, then add the parmesan, butter and chopped spinach. Correct the seasoning.

On a flat grill or in a non-stick pan, pan-fry the snapper fillets skin-side down, then turn to finish cooking (3–4 minutes).

To serve

Place a serving of risotto in the centre of each plate and top with a snapper fillet. Place a nut of brown butter on top, or pour on a dressing of Chardonnay vinegar and olive oil.

An ideal accompaniment is finely sliced pancetta, char-grilled with radicchio and lemon olive oil.

Serves 6

Recipe from Chris Taylor
FRASER'S RESTAURANT
PERTH

Recommended wine:
Rosily Margaret River
Semillon/Sauvignon Blanc 2005

RIGHT: Camels have been used as riding and pack animals in the arid areas of Central and Western Australia since 1840. Some were abandoned, and these feral camels bred prolifically and are now estimated to number more than 500,000.

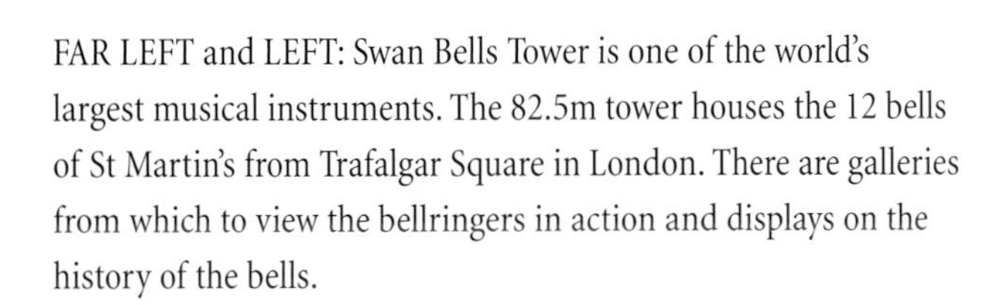

FAR LEFT and LEFT: Swan Bells Tower is one of the world's largest musical instruments. The 82.5m tower houses the 12 bells of St Martin's from Trafalgar Square in London. There are galleries from which to view the bellringers in action and displays on the history of the bells.

BELOW: Greg James had his first solo exhibition in 1978. Today his sculptures, including *Pear 2*, a stylised bronze work with art deco elements, are landmarks around Perth and Fremantle.

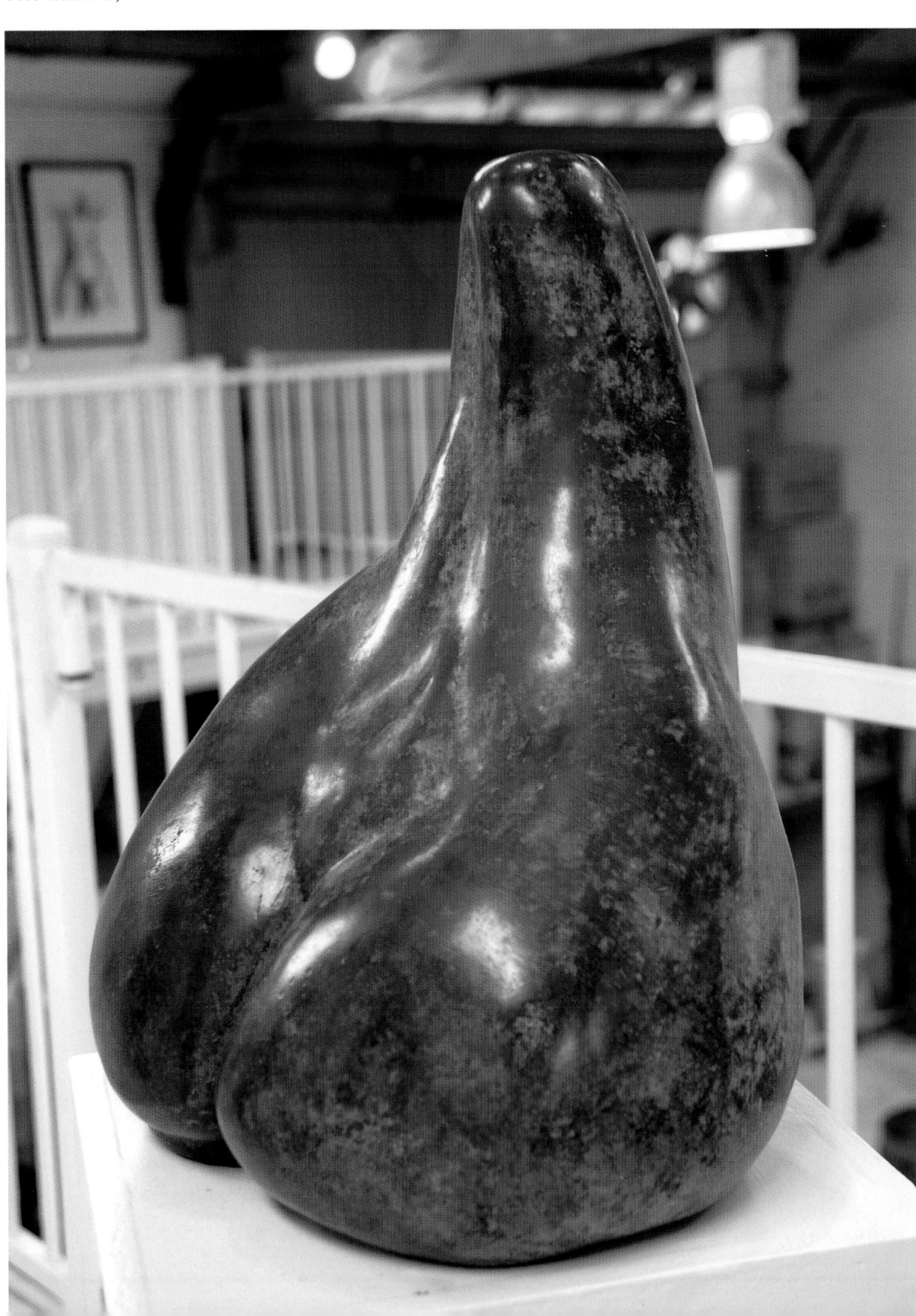

ABOVE: *Far Out Homestead,* an acrylic on canvas by Keith Bromfield.

Spicy Salmon

with spring onion mash and ratatouille vegetables

4 x 180g salmon fillets, skin on
3 tablespoons extra virgin olive oil
400g potatoes, peeled and diced
1 cup finely sliced spring onion
1 tablespoon wholeseed mustard
salt flakes
freshly ground black pepper
½ cup finely sliced shallots
2 cloves garlic, peeled and finely sliced
1 teaspoon fresh thyme leaves
2 tablespoons mustard seed oil
½ cup sweet sherry
70ml vegetable stock
1 yellow capsicum
2 red capsicums
1 small eggplant
1 green zucchini
2 tablespoons butter, melted
chilli flakes to taste

Preheat the oven to 180°C. Seal the salmon skin-side down for 1–2 minutes over a medium heat in a non-stick pan with 1 tablespoon of the extra virgin olive oil until the skin is crisp and golden. Turn over and seal the fleshy side for 1–2 minutes. Remove from the pan, place on a tray lined with greaseproof paper, and set aside.

Boil the potatoes in salted water, then drain and mash with a fork. Mix in the spring onion, mustard and remaining olive oil. Season to taste and place in a microwaveable container.

In a non-stick pan gently fry the shallots, garlic and thyme in the mustard seed oil until soft. Add sherry and reduce by half. Add the stock. Reduce by half again. Blend the mixture and pass through a sieve. Set aside.

Wash the capsicums, eggplant and zucchini, and remove the seeds and stalks. Cut eight 2cm-square pieces of each vegetable. Set aside for garnish.

To finish and serve

Put the salmon in the oven for 5 minutes. Blanch the capsicum, eggplant and zucchini garnish in boiling, salted water for 1 minute, then remove. Glaze with melted butter. Heat the potato mash in the microwave.

Spoon the mash onto the centre of each plate. Alternate the vegetables around the plate. Place a salmon fillet on each serving of mash and pour the sauce around.

Serves 4

Recipe from: Richard Selfe
FRIENDS RESTAURANT
EAST PERTH

Recommended wine:

Leeuwin Estate Art Series
Margaret River Sauvignon Blanc 2005

Chocolate Jaffa Mousse

layered with mud cake

JAFFA MOUSSE

zest of 2 oranges
200ml milk
4 egg yolks
100g caster sugar
50ml orange juice
150g dark chocolate, melted
1 teaspoon gelatine
300ml cream, whipped
6 cylindrical moulds, greased
chocolate mud cake, cut into 1cm-thick rounds to fit moulds
250g block milk chocolate
transparency sheets (available from office stationers), cut into six 15cm-sided triangles

Steep the zest in the milk. Whisk the yolks and sugar until light and fluffy. Add the milk mixture and orange juice and gently heat. Stir until thickened then remove from the heat. Add the melted chocolate and gelatine and mix well. Strain through a sieve. Allow to cool. When cold, but not set, fold the whipped cream through.

Stand the moulds on a tray lined with greaseproof paper. Pour the mousse into the moulds and top each with a round of mud cake. Refrigerate for 2 hours, then take out and remove the moulds.

Melt the milk chocolate. Spread thinly onto the transparency triangles one at a time, then wrap around each mousse and refrigerate.

ORANGE CARAMEL

300g caster sugar
100ml water
150ml orange juice
zest of 3 oranges

Boil the sugar and water until it turns a caramel colour. Add the orange juice and zest, then boil for 10 minutes. Remove from the heat and allow to cool.

SPUN SUGAR
200g caster sugar
100ml water

Combine the sugar and water in a saucepan and stir over low heat. Remove from the heat when just turning golden, then cool slightly. Take spoonfuls of the sugar and drizzle thin strands onto a large sheet of greaseproof paper. As these cool and set, pick up handfuls and roll into balls.

To finish and serve
white and dark chocolate, melted

Pipe dark chocolate outlines to the shape of a butterfly wing. Allow to set. Fill in with white chocolate then allow to set. Join the butterfly wings together with dark chocolate. Repeat 5 times.

Pipe a leaf shape onto each plate with melted chocolate. When set, fill in the leaves with orange caramel. Place a jaffa mousse on each plate and carefully remove the transparency sheets from chocolate. Place a spun sugar ball on top of each mousse, then place a butterfly alongside.

Serves 6

Recipe from: Alexis Jackson
FRIENDS RESTAURANT
EAST PERTH

Recommended wine:
Talijancich Reserve Muscat Blend No 1
1961 Swan Valley

RIGHT: *The Magic Tree*. This fantasy sculpture, which depicts a tree that has morphed into a variety of animals, is a galvanised and treated steel work by Coral Lowry.

FOLLOWING PAGE: Bringing a new meaning to 'living on the water' – houses built on a pier in Busselton.

Stuffed Pheasant and Quail Breast

with sun-dried tomatoes, smoked ham, provolone and Tuscan pesto

PHEASANT

100g smoked ham
100g sun-dried tomatoes
50g aged provolone cheese (available from delis)
1 sprig thyme
¼ cup chopped flat-leaved parsley
1 pheasant breast, skin on and butterflied
pinch of salt
pinch of cracked black pepper
thyme and rosemary sprigs for roasting
extra virgin olive oil for drizzling

Blend the ham, tomatoes and cheese to make a coarse mixture. Add thyme and parsley. Spoon a little mixture in the centre of the breast and close back to original shape. Season and place on a baking tray layered with thyme and rosemary sprigs. Drizzle with extra virgin olive oil. Roast (the chef does this in a wood-fired oven) for 5–6 minutes. Allow to rest for 5 minutes in a warm spot before serving.

QUAIL BREAST

1 double quail breast, deboned
pinch of salt
cracked black pepper
2 green asparagus spears, peeled
2 thin slices pancetta
extra virgin olive oil for drizzling
1 tablespoon Tuscan pesto (see 'Recipes Continued' on page 190)

Season the quail breast skin-side down, place the asparagus in the centre of the breast lengthwise, roll up and wrap with pancetta. Season with cracked black pepper and drizzle with extra virgin olive oil. Place on a baking tray and roast in a wood-fired oven for 5–6 minutes.

Brush the quail breast with pesto. Allow to rest for 5–6 minutes before serving.

POTATOES

200g potatoes, peeled, cubed and boiled
1 onion, sliced and sautéed until browned
1 bay leaf
50ml extra virgin olive oil
pinch of salt
pinch of cracked black pepper
1 sprig thyme
1 clove garlic, peeled and minced

Gently cook the potatoes, onion and bay leaf in oil until the potatoes start to turn golden and crisp. Season and add thyme and garlic. Keep warm.

To serve

Spoon the warm potatoes in the centre of a plate. Top with the pheasant breast then the quail breast. Drizzle pesto all around the potatoes and serve with reduced pheasant or chicken stock.

Serves 1

Recipe from: Vincenzo Soresi
GALILEO BUONA CUCINA
PERTH

Recommended wine:

Juniper Estate Margaret River
Cabernet Sauvignon 2002

BELOW: *Grape Sucking Sirene*, a cast bronze by Greg James.

Salmon-wrapped Russian Salad

with quail eggs, grilled tuna and baby capers

CURED SALMON

1/3 cup sugar
1/2 cup sea salt
600g side fresh Tasmanian salmon, skin on, scaled and pin bones removed
2 tablespoons extra virgin olive oil
1 teaspoon lemon pepper
zest of 1/2 lemon

Mix together the sugar and salt. Sprinkle a thin layer onto a non-corrosive tray with high sides. Place the salmon skin-side down and cover the surface with the remaining sugar and salt. Cover with plastic cling film and refrigerate for 12 hours.

Rinse the salt mixture off the salmon and dry with a clean cloth. Brush oil on the flesh, and sprinkle with lemon pepper and zest. Press the seasonings gently with your hand so they adhere to the salmon. Slice very thinly with a sharp carving knife as needed.

BOILED QUAIL EGGS

4 quail eggs
vinegar

Boil the quail eggs in water with a little vinegar. Peel carefully. Set aside.

TUNA

160g tuna, cut into cubes
4 caperberries
salt and freshly ground black pepper
150ml lemon juice
150ml extra virgin olive oil

Thread the tuna cubes and caperberries onto four 12cm-long bamboo skewers. Season with salt and pepper. Brush with the combined lemon and oil, and grill on a char-grill for 15 seconds each side or until cooked rare.

RUSSIAN SALAD

1 large carrot, srubbed and diced
1 medium potato, peeled and diced
8 fresh stringless green beans
200g prawns, shelled
200g scallops
3 medium mushrooms, diced and sautéed in oil and garlic
salt and freshly ground black pepper
Tabasco sauce and lemon juice to taste
3/4 cup mayonnaise (see 'Recipes Continued' on page 190)

Boil the carrot, potato and beans in salted water until tender. Add the prawns and scallops and boil for 1 minute further. Strain well and chill in a colander.

Add the mushrooms to the mixture and season to taste with salt, pepper, Tabasco and lemon juice. Mix in the mayonnaise to make a firm salad.

To serve

sea salt flakes
mixed salad leaves
balsamic vinaigrette (see 'Recipes Continued' on page 190)
baby capers
1 lemon, cut into wedges

Spoon the salad into a 5cm-diameter cutter ring on one side of each plate. Remove the ring and wrap salmon slices around the salad mould. Top with a quail egg cut in 2. Season with sea salt flakes. Place mixed salad leaves on the other side of each plate and drizzle with balsamic vinaigrette. Sprinkle baby capers around the salads. Top the salad leaves with a char-grilled tuna skewer. Serve with a lemon wedge.

Serves 4

Recipe from: Vincenzo Soresi
GALILEO BUONA CUCINA
PERTH

Recommended wine:
Ashbrook Estate Margaret River Semillon 2005

RAMS
A Better Way.
Call 13RAMS
HIRE
BERRYMAN

ABOVE: Yachts racing on the Swan River with Perth city in the background.

Rabbit in Prosciutto

with beetroot risotto

RABBIT IN PROSCIUTTO

1 small red onion, peeled and chopped
3 cloves garlic, peeled and chopped
olive oil
1 sprig fresh thyme
100g chestnuts, cooked, peeled and chopped
salt and freshly ground black pepper
8 slices prosciutto
2 rabbit loins (4 boneless back fillets)

Preheat the oven to 190°C. Over a medium heat, sweat the onion and the garlic in a little olive oil, without letting it brown. When soft, add the thyme leaves and chestnuts. Cook for a further 2 minutes, season with salt and pepper, remove from the heat and set aside to cool. Lay out the prosciutto on a tea towel, slightly overlapping, to form a square sheet as wide as the rabbit fillets.

Place 2 rabbit fillets on one edge of the prosciutto, spoon on the chestnut mixture and place the remaining fillets on top. Roll up in the prosciutto to form a log, then place on a roasting tray, brush with a little olive oil and cook in the oven for 15 minutes. Remove and keep warm.

BEETROOT RISOTTO

1 small red onion, peeled and chopped
50ml olive oil
160g arborio rice
100ml red wine
600ml beetroot juice
1 beetroot, peeled, diced and roasted
120g horseradish cream (4 tablespoons horseradish and 5 tablespoons cream)
75g parmesan, grated
50g butter
salt and freshly ground black pepper

Sweat the onion in the oil, then add the rice to sweat until hot. Do not brown. Stir in the red wine until absorbed. Bring the beetroot juice to the boil and skim off any froth. Pour the juice over the rice and bring back to the boil, then simmer for 6 minutes. Strain, reserving the beetroot juice. Mix the roasted beetroot with the rice. Spread on a tray to cool.

Place the rice and beetroot juice in a saucepan and bring to the boil, stirring continuously. Turn the heat to medium and continue to stir. When the juice has been absorbed, remove from the heat and stir in 1 tablespoon of the horseradish cream, the cheese and butter. Season to taste.

To serve
Slice the rabbit. Spoon the risotto into bowls, place the rabbit on top and drizzle with the remaining horseradish cream.

Serves 4

Recipe from Neal Jackson
JACKSON'S RESTAURANT
PERTH

Recommended wine:
Talijancich Swan Valley
Graciano 2003

LEFT:
Star Anise is a crayon on paper work by Pat Shields.

Caramelised Pork Belly

with star fruit, marron and fragrant herb salad

CHINESE MASTER STOCK

4 litres water
750ml light soy sauce
150ml dark soy sauce
750ml Chinese rice wine (available from Asian food stores)
1½ cups crushed yellow rock sugar (available from Asian food stores)
200g ginger, peeled and sliced
10 spring onions, sliced
1 teaspoon Szechuan pepper
8 star anise
4 cassia sticks (or cinnamon)
6 pieces dried tangerine peel

Place all the ingredients in a large saucepan, bring to the boil, then reduce the heat and simmer for 15 minutes.

PALM SUGAR CARAMEL

⅓ cup shaved palm sugar
1 tablespoon water
1 teaspoon fish sauce
½ cassia stick (or cinnamon)
1 star anise
50ml kecap manis
50g pineapple, coarsely chopped

Melt the palm sugar in a pan with the water and fish sauce. Add the cassia stick and star anise and cook over a medium heat until a dark caramel is formed. Stop the process by adding kecap manis and removing from the heat. Add the pineapple and return to a low heat to infuse for 5 minutes. Pass the caramel through a fine sieve.

CARAMELISED PORK BELLY AND MARRON

3 live marron (or fresh tiger prawns)
1kg pork belly, deboned
vegetable oil for deep-frying

SALAD

¼ cup coriander leaves
¼ cup mint leaves
¼ cup Thai basil
¼ cup Vietnamese mint
¼ cup rice paddy herb leaves (available from Asian food stores)
1 star fruit, sliced
1 Lebanese cucumber, deseeded and sliced
1 large red chilli, julienned
1 shallot, shaved
1 tablespoon roasted peanuts, chopped
1 tablespoon fried shallots (available from Asian food stores)
nahm jim dressing (see 'Recipes Continued' on page 190)

Poach the marron in boiling, salted water for 5 minutes and refresh in iced water. Remove the flesh from the tail and claws and slice.

Bring the master stock to the boil in a saucepan that will accommodate the pork belly. Poach the pork belly in the stock for 90 minutes or until the pork feels tender. Some weight may be required to prevent the pork floating above the surface.

Remove the pork from the stock, press between 2 flat trays and refrigerate for 10 hours. You will need 2–3kg of weight to press the pork flat. Score the skin of the pressed pork about 1mm deep with a sharp knife. Cut into 2cm cubes.

To finish and serve

Heat the oil in a deep-fryer to 180°C and fry the pork until the fat layers become golden. Drain well on kitchen paper, then coat generously with the warm palm sugar caramel and arrange on plates.

Toss all the salad ingredients with the marron in a bowl. Dress generously with nahm jim dressing. Arrange the salad on top of the caramelised pork. Drizzle extra caramel and nahm jim on and around the salad.

Serves 4

Recipe from David Coomer
STAR ANISE
PERTH

Recommended wine:

Victory Point Margaret River Chardonnay 2005

ABOVE: Margaret River was the setting for *Bentley Drivers Club*, an acrylic and oil on board work by Len Zuks. It depicts a moment in the 2004 Bentley Rally in which the artist drove the silver and red car.

Vincotto-dressed Beetroot Salad

with green beans and Roy de Valles cheese

50g mixed leaves (Swiss chard, wild rocket, baby lettuce)
50ml extra virgin olive oil
salt and freshly ground black pepper
10 stringless green beans, sliced lengthwise
6 baby beetroot (cleaned, boiled, peeled, topped and tailed, and halved)
20g Roy de Valles cheese
50ml fig vincotto (available from delis)

Place the leaves in a bowl and dress with half the olive oil, then season. Place a neat pile of the leaves in the centre of each plate. In the same mixing bowl toss the beans, then place on the leaves. Dress the beetroot with 3/4 of the vincotto and place the leaves alongside.

Shave the cheese and scatter the shavings on top. Drizzle the remainder of the olive oil on the leaves, cheese and plate, then do the same with the vincotto.

NOTE: Roy de Valles is made in the fertile valleys of the Pyrénées, France, where the local shepherds have made their ewe's milk cheeses famous. Understanding the precious qualities of both goat's and ewe's milk, the makers have combined the milks to produce this cheese. Matured for 9–12 months, this artisan hard-cooked cheese displays the smooth, full texture of the ewe's milk, while the goat's milk provides acidity and a lingering, piquant flavour.

Serves 2

Recipe from Brad Burton
SUBIACO HOTEL
PERTH

Recommended wine:
Pierro Margaret River
Semillon/Sauvignon Blanc 2005

BELOW: *Mist 2* is a stylised bronze with art deco elements by Greg James.

Martabak Spicy Beef Roti

with quail eggs and yellow curry sauce

YELLOW CURRY SAUCE

2 tablespoons oil
bones from 4 large chickens
10 cloves garlic, peeled
4 onions, peeled and sliced
6 sticks lemongrass, sliced
2 tablespoons ground turmeric
2 x 400ml cans coconut cream
salt and white pepper

In a large saucepan heat a little oil and brown the chicken bones, garlic, onions and lemongrass over a low heat, stirring regularly, until nicely browned.

Add the turmeric and stir in well. Add the coconut cream and season with salt and white pepper. Bring to the boil and simmer for 30 minutes. Pass through a fine sieve.

MARTABAK PASTRY

125g flour
1/2 teaspoon salt
60ml water
2 tablespoons vegetable oil
125ml vegetable oil, extra

Place the flour and salt in a bowl and pour in the water and oil. Mix to a dough and divide into 50g portions. Form each portion into a ball about the size of a golf ball and roll in the extra oil.

MARTABAK FILLING

1/4 onion, peeled and finely chopped
1/4 tablespoon oil
1/4 teaspoon crushed garlic
125g beef mince
sea salt and freshly ground black pepper
1 egg
bunch of spring onions, chopped

Fry the onion in a pan with the oil. Add the garlic, beef mince, and 1/4 teaspoon each of salt and pepper. Continue frying until beef is cooked.

Place the egg in a bowl. Add the spring onions, a pinch of salt, a pinch of pepper and the mince mixture. Mix together.

To finish and serve

12 quail eggs, boiled and peeled

Roll each ball of pastry into a 15cm square. Put 2 tablespoons of filling in the centre, wrap like an envelope and fry until browned. Place in a 160°C oven for 10 minutes to finish off. Place the quail eggs in the yellow curry sauce and warm through.

Serve the martabak on a plate with the yellow curry sauce and quail eggs to one side, garnished with spring onions.

Serves 4

Recipe from Brad Burton
SUBIACO HOTEL
PERTH

Recommended wine:
Edwards Margaret River Shiraz 2004

Where the vine reigns supreme

South Australia

LOVE RED WINE? Then visit South Australia – the country's biggest wine producer by a considerable margin, this heat-baked state has put 'Aussie Shiraz' on the world wine map.

The purple-coloured grape, known elsewhere in the world as Syrah, has found its spiritual home in the local dry, dusty soils, producing mouth-filling rich wines that are a must on the table and in the cellar of any serious enthusiast.

Production is centred in the Barossa Valley, home to the most famous example of them all. Penfolds Grange is the only wine in the country to achieve recognition as an international superstar. It sells for hundreds of dollars on release, and single bottles from the 1950s have sold at auction for more than $50 000.

Where wine is taken that seriously, so must be food, thus it is no accident that this far-spread state boasts plenty of good eating.

The best chefs in Adelaide and its satellite coastal townships concentrate on presenting local ingredients in original ways, but the large immigrant population over the years has meant that the dozens of Italian, Greek, Vietnamese, Thai, Cantonese and other specialist establishments are all well patronised.

The immigrants have also brought a unique atmosphere to small towns around the state, with architectural features from many parts of the world contributing to the local character. Adelaide itself boasts many meticulously maintained Victorian buildings, particularly near Rundle Mall, the city's main shopping precinct. After hours, Hindley Street at the mall's western end is home to vibrant nightclubs and Middle Eastern cafés.

Cultural influences are strong, as a visit to the Art Gallery of South Australia will show. Among the exhibits is the world's largest collection of Western Desert paintings.

And for culture of a totally different sort, visit the Adelaide Casino. South Australia really does have something for everybody!

LEFT: Century-old Shiraz vines growing at Seppeltsfield, one of the oldest wine-producing communities in the Barossa Valley.

Terrarossa Tenderloin

dusted with porcini, with polenta cake, celeriac and Pinot Noir jus

POLENTA CAKE

2 tablespoons chopped onion
25g butter
200ml milk
50g mascarpone
200g polenta
2 tablespoons chopped flat-leaf parsley
½ cup finely grated parmesan

Sweat the onion in the butter. Add the milk and mascarpone, and bring to the boil. Pour in the polenta and cook for about 5 minutes, stirring all the time. Add the parsley and parmesan. Pour into a lightly greased 5cm-deep pan and pat down with wet hands to smooth. When cold, cut with a small cutter.

CELERIAC PURÉE

1 celeriac, peeled and diced
150ml milk
1 bay leaf

Cook the celeriac in the milk with the bay leaf. When tender, strain and blend until very smooth.

PINOT NOIR JUS

½ onion, peeled and chopped
½ carrot, chopped
½ celery stick, chopped
1 tablespoon chopped fresh thyme
¼ cup beef trimmings
1 x 250ml glass Pinot Noir
½ litre beef stock

Sauté vegetables and thyme until browned. Add the beef trimmings and deglaze the pan with the wine. Reduce by 3/4 then add the stock and cook for 45 minutes. Strain.

SPINACH PURÉE AND STUFFED TOMATO

2 bunches spinach
1 zucchini, sliced
1 sprig basil
3 cherry tomatoes

Blanch half the spinach then blend. Mix with a soup spoon of celeriac purée and set aside.

Sauté the zucchini with the basil and the remaining bunch of spinach and blend. Cut the cherry tomatoes in half and remove flesh. Fill tomato shells with the spinach mix. There may be some mixture left over.

TERRAROSSA TENDERLOIN

850g Terrarossa beef tenderloin
30g porcini powder
20ml olive oil
chopped parsley to garnish

Preheat the oven to 200°C. Cut beef into 5 portions. Dip one side of the steaks in porcini powder, then sear both sides in a pan in hot oil. Place in the oven for 5 minutes.

To serve

Place on a plate a polenta cake, top with a portion of beef, sprinkle with chopped parsley and drizzle some jus around.

To one side spoon some spinach purée and place a stuffed tomato on top. On the other side, place a spoonful of celeriac purée.

Serves 5

Recipe from: Jerome Tremoulet
MAGILL ESTATE RESTAURANT
MAGILL

Recommended wine:
Penfolds Grange 1995

BELOW: Chris Angrave, a young Aboriginal artist, painted *Gudungalla (Crab)*. It is acrylic on canvas and depicts a hunting trail of the blue swimmer crab.

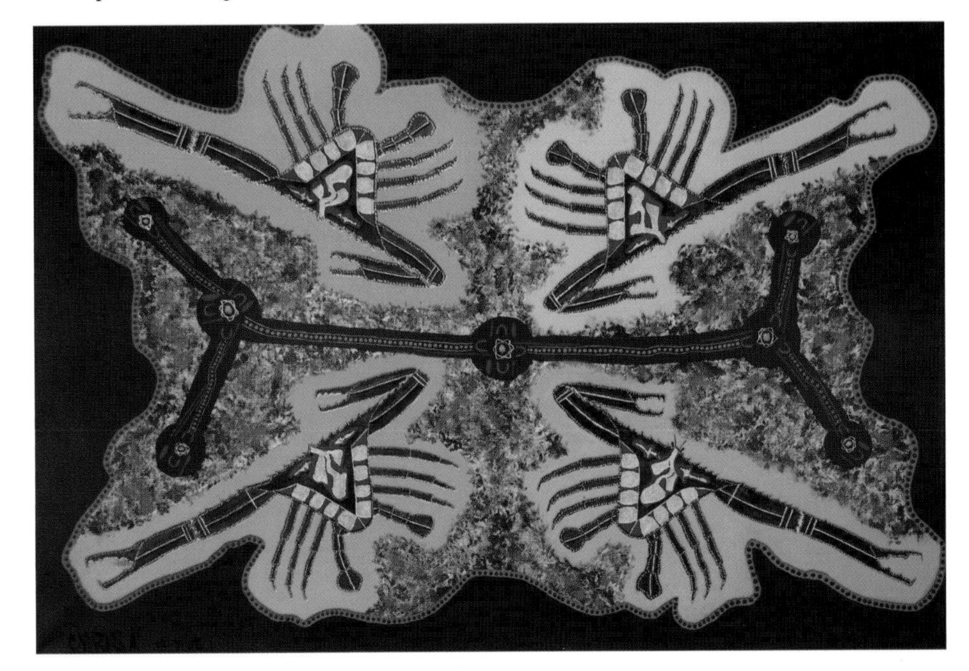

LEFT: Alexander Brun painted *Australiana 2* in oil on canvas and it is now permanently displayed at the Barossa Regional Gallery.

Kangaroo Island Yabby Tails

with crayfish timbale and tarragon pesto

CONFIT TOMATOES

2 1/2 beef tomatoes, blanched, deseeded and quartered
20ml olive oil
20g sugar
10g thyme leaves
1 clove garlic, peeled and finely sliced

Preheat the oven to 80°C. Toss the tomato pieces in olive oil, place on a baking sheet, sprinkle with sugar and thyme, and place a sliver of garlic on each. Bake for 2–2 1/2 hours.

TARRAGON PESTO

6 cloves confit garlic (peel and cook very slowly in vegetable oil until tender)
1 bunch basil
1 bunch tarragon
100g parmesan
100g pine nuts
200ml olive oil
200ml vegetable oil

Process all ingredients in a blender until smooth.

RED CAPSICUM REDUCTION

8 red capsicums, cored and deseeded
200ml vegetable oil

Juice the capsicums in a juicer. Place in a saucepan and reduce until nearly syrup (change the saucepan occasionally if starting to catch). Allow to cool. When cold, blend slowly with the vegetable oil until very thick.

CRAYFISH TIMBALE

1 crayfish tail
1 litre vegetable stock (see 'Recipes Continued' on page 191)
1 tablespoon olive oil
1 teaspoon chopped tarragon
salt and freshly ground black pepper
1 avocado, peeled and diced
juice of 1 lemon
1 zucchini, thinly sliced lengthwise and blanched
5 flat-leaf parsley leaves
2/3 cup microgreens

Add the crayfish tail to the vegetable stock and cook for 6 minutes. Remove from the stock, then peel and dice very finely and mix with the olive oil, chopped tarragon and salt and pepper.

Mix the avocado with the lemon juice and salt.

Line each of five 45mm plastic rings with a blanched slice of zucchini. Place one piece of confit tomato at the base of each ring, half fill with avocado, then add another piece of confit tomato. Fill to the top with crayfish mixture and top with another piece of confit tomato.

To finish and serve

10 Kangaroo Island yabby tails, cooked
chervil to garnish

Place the timbale on a plate and remove the plastic ring. Stick a blanched parsley leaf on the tomato. Dress the microgreens and place on top of the timbale.

Garnish each plate with 2 yabby tails dressed in lemon and chervil, and a small spoonful of tarragon pesto and a little red capsicum reduction.

Serves 5

Recipe from: Jerome Tremoulet
MAGILL ESTATE RESTAURANT
MAGILL

Recommended wine:

Penfolds Bin 311 Tumbarumba Chardonnay 2005

Loin of Venison

with braised lentils, pumpkin purée and beetroot glaze

Each element in this recipe can be prepared in advance, then reheated when required.

BRAISED LENTILS

½ cup small green lentils
¼ cup finely diced carrot
¼ cup finely diced celery
¼ cup finely diced onion
1 tablespoon butter
250ml reduced meat stock
½ teaspoon thyme leaves
1 teaspoon red wine vinegar
2 tablespoons chopped parsley
salt and freshly ground black pepper

Cover the lentils with water and simmer until tender and the liquid is absorbed. Sauté the vegetables in butter until soft, then add the lentils, stock and thyme. Simmer until well reduced and almost sticky. Add the vinegar and parsley, season to taste and set aside.

BEETROOT GLAZE

8 shallots, peeled and finely chopped
¼ cup finely diced carrots
¼ cup finely diced celery
1 sprig thyme
20 peppercorns, crushed
125ml red wine
1 teaspoon red wine vinegar
1 litre reduced game stock
1 teaspoon redcurrant jelly
20 juniper berries, crushed
4 cooked beetroot, finely diced
salt and freshly ground black pepper

Place the vegetables in a saucepan with the thyme, peppercorns, wine and vinegar, and reduce until almost dry. Add the stock, reduce to 300ml and set aside. Just before serving add the jelly, juniper berries and beetroot. Infuse (do not boil or the colour will fade). Check the seasoning and strain.

PUMPKIN PURÉE

250g butternut pumpkin, peeled and cut into large pieces
50g butter
30ml cream
salt, freshly ground black pepper and nutmeg to taste

Preheat the oven to 180°C. Steam the pumpkin until tender. Drain and place on a tray lined with baking paper and roast in the oven until dried off and lightly coloured. Purée with the butter and cream, season and keep warm.

VENISON

600g loin of venison (150g per person), trimmed of fat and sinew
butter for frying
salt and freshly ground black pepper

Slice the venison into 50g medallions and flatten lightly to a thickness of about 1cm. Set aside.

Place butter in a hot frying pan and seal the venison for 1 minute on each side. Season the meat and allow to rest in a warm place for 5 minutes.

To serve

4 cooked baby beets and fine cress for garnish

Place a mound of the pumpkin purée in the centre of each plate, make a well in the centre and spoon in the warmed lentils. Stack the venison medallions on top and spoon the glaze over.

Garnish with cooked baby beets and fine cress.

Serves 4

Recipe from: Mark McNamara
APPELLATION RESTAURANT
AT PEPPERS THE LOUISE
TANUNDA

Recommended wine:
Hutton Vale Eden Valley
Grenache/Mataro 2004

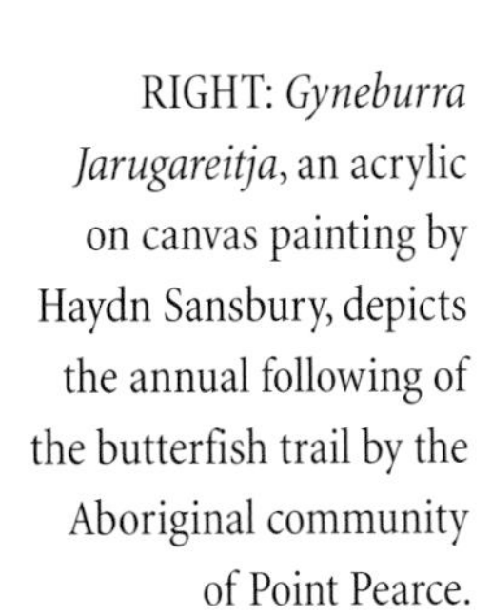

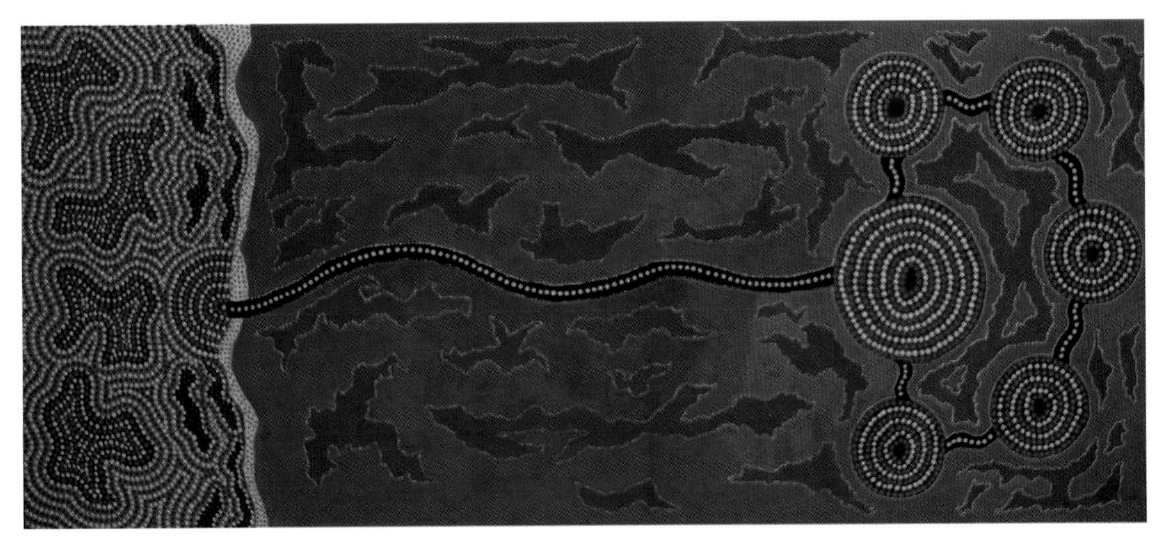

RIGHT: *Gyneburra Jarugareitja*, an acrylic on canvas painting by Haydn Sansbury, depicts the annual following of the butterfish trail by the Aboriginal community of Point Pearce.

Barossa Corn-fed Chicken

and lachsschinken with garlic and sage glaze

The secret to this recipe is to prepare the sauce to stage three ahead of time and, most importantly, to cook the chicken on the lowest possible heat until just set.

GARLIC AND SAGE GLAZE

2 chicken wings, chopped into 1cm pieces
1/3 cup finely chopped onion
1/4 cup white wine
1 tablespoon verjuice
4 cups chicken stock
8 sage leaves
2 cloves garlic, peeled and sliced

Lightly brown the chicken and onion in a non-stick pan without oil, taking care not to burn. Add the wine and verjuice to deglaze the pan, then add the stock and simmer for 20 minutes. Strain the stock, skim off any fat, then add the garlic and sage, and reduce to 1/2 cup. Strain again and reserve.

ROASTED VEGETABLES

1 medium potato, peeled and cut into crescent shapes
1 medium sweet potato, peeled and cut into crescent shapes
8 whole cloves garlic, peeled
1 tablespoon olive oil
salt and freshly ground black pepper

Preheat the oven to 180ºC. Toss all the potato and garlic in oil with seasoning, wrap in tinfoil and bake until tender. Open the foil and continue to bake until browned. Keep warm.

BUTTER-POACHED CHICKEN

4 chicken breasts
70g butter
1 clove garlic, peeled and sliced
4 sage leaves
8 slices lachsschinken
50g cold butter, cut into 1cm dice

Remove the tendons and fat. Slice each breast into 3 thin escallops. Flatten all 12 pieces between plastic cling film to a thickness of about 4mm. Heat the butter in a large frying pan (do not allow to brown), reduce the heat and add the garlic and sage then the chicken and gently cook until just set.

Remove the chicken and keep warm. Add the sliced lachsschinken to the pan and warm gently.

Bring the reserved glaze back to the boil, reduce the heat to low and add the second measure of butter, a piece at a time, whisking constantly until glossy. Keep warm. Do not reboil or the sauce will separate.

To serve

Place the vegetables on plates, alternate layers of the chicken and lachsschinken, placing a little sauce on each layer. Dress with remaining sauce. Garnish with sage leaves and serve immediately.

Serves 4

Recipe from: Mark McNamara
APPELLATION RESTAURANT
AT PEPPERS THE LOUISE
TANUNDA

Recommended wine:
Heathvale Eden Valley
Chardonnay 2005

ABOVE: Glenelg is the most popular and easily accessible of Adelaide's beaches.

Pig's Trotters

with chicken mousseline on mashed potato with cos lettuce

TROTTERS

4 pig's trotters, boned
2 small carrots, scrubbed and diced
1 medium onion, peeled and diced
2 large stalks celery, diced
150ml red wine
2 tablespoons ruby port
500ml brown veal stock

Preheat the oven to 180°C. Place all the ingredients in a casserole. Cover and braise in the oven for 3 ½ hours.

CHICKEN MOUSSELINE

600g cooked chicken breast
1 egg white
200ml thick cream
sea salt and ground white pepper
2 tablespoons mixture of finely chopped flat-leaf parsley, tarragon and chervil

Dice the chicken breast and purée with the egg white and cream. Season with salt and white pepper. Mix in the herbs and set aside.

MASHED POTATO

2 large potatoes, peeled
30ml thick cream
150g butter
salt and freshly ground black pepper

Cook the potatoes in boiling, salted water for about 25 minutes, strain and mash while still hot. In a saucepan boil the cream, add the potato and butter and mix thoroughly. Season with salt and pepper to taste.

To finish and serve

8 cos lettuces leaves, washed

Remove the trotters from the casserole and strain the cooking juices, reserving the liquid and discarding the vegetables. Open out the trotters flat and place each on a piece of buttered tinfoil. Leave to cool.

Fill the cooled trotters with the chicken mousseline and roll tightly in the tinfoil. Refrigerate for 3 hours.

Bring a medium saucepan with about 8cm of water to the boil. Carefully place the foil-wrapped trotters in the pan. Cover and steam for 15–20 minutes, turning once.

Meanwhile, pour the reserved cooking juices into a clean pan and reduce over a high heat to a shiny coating consistency. Correct the seasoning with salt and pepper and finish with a little butter if desired.

Place a serving of mashed potato in the centre of each plate, unwrap the trotters and place on top. Pour a little sauce over each. Place 2 cos leaves beside each trotter and serve.

Serves 4

Recipe from Ayhan Erkol
SALOPIAN INN
McLAREN VALE

Recommended wine:
Gemtree Bloodstone
McLaren Vale Tempranillo 2005

RIGHT: *Talking Our Way Home* – paper boats on the River Torrens by Shaun Kirby.

Winery
2003

ABOVE: This woven wool hanging, *Woven Recital*, by Katharina Urban and pupils of the Barossa weavers, depicts some of the history of the Barossa Valley.

Eye Fillet Steak on Parmesan

and potato rösti with roast mushroom crumble and condiments

4 potatoes, peeled
melted butter
1 cup grated parmesan plus an extra 2 tablespoons
1x 250g tenderloin eye fillet steak
vegetable oil for frying
2 medium field mushrooms
olive oil
salt and freshly ground black pepper
1 onion, peeled and finely diced
1/3 cup fresh white breadcrumbs
2 tablespoons chopped parsley
4 tablespoons of your favourite 4 condiments (e.g. English mustard, horseradish cream, red pesto, black olive tapenade, or any vegetable purée)

Grate the potato into a bowl and squeeze out all the excess starch and juice. Mix in a little melted butter to stop the potato discolouring. Add 1 cup grated parmesan and mix thoroughly. Lightly oil and heat a flat non-stick frying pan to a low temperature, place mounds of the potato mix in the pan and push down on them slightly to form flat discs. Allow the potato to brown gently before turning and cooking the other side. Fry until crisp.

Drizzle one mushroom with olive oil and season with salt and pepper. Roast in the oven at 200°C for 10 minutes. Chop the other mushroom very finely and fry in a little olive oil over a medium heat with the onion until the mix is quite dark and becomes a paste. Season to taste.

Mix the breadcrumbs, remaining parmesan and parsley together. Top the roasted mushroom with the diced mushroom and onion mix, then the breadcrumb mix and roast in the oven until golden brown. Oil and season the steak and grill or seal in a frying pan on a high heat to your liking.

To serve
Place the rösti in the middle of the plate and top with the steak. Carefully mould 4 tablespoons of condiments around the rösti and place the mushroom crumble on the steak.

Serves 1

Recipe from Peter Burrows
COS RESTAURANT
ADELAIDE

Recommended wine:
Veritas 'Bulls Blood' Shiraz/Mataro Pressings 2003

Rasam Eggplant Timbales

12 eggs, beaten
100ml Dijon mustard
30ml white balsamic vinegar
2 lemons and white pepper
2 teaspoons rasam curry powder (South Indian)
2 eggplants, char-grilled, deseeded and flesh finely chopped
400ml cream

Preheat the oven to 150°C. Strain the eggs through a fine chinois or sieve to remove the white strings surrounding the yolk, then combine all the ingredients. Grease 6 timbale moulds and fill each to a third with the mixture. Place the timbales in a water bath, cover with plastic cling film with several perforations and steam for about 30 minutes until set.

ZUCCHINI CHIPS
1 zucchini, finely sliced into half rounds (preferably with a mandolin)
150ml dosa batter (available from Indian food stores)
2 1/2 tablespoons wheat starch
1/4 teaspoon fungus-free baking powder
oil for deep-frying
sea salt and rasam curry powder

Combine all the ingredients and tempura fry in hot oil. Season the chips with sea salt and rasam curry powder.

BROAD BEAN PURÉE
200g dried broad beans, soaked overnight (remove from outer casing)
2 white onions, peeled and thinly sliced
4 roma tomatoes, cut in quarters and deseeded
2 fresh bay leaves
soda water
200ml white wine, heated to burn the alcohol away
150ml olive oil
200g tahini
salt and freshly ground black pepper

Simmer the beans, onion, tomato and bay leaves until tender in the wine and enough soda water to cover, covered with a cartouche (greaseproof paper cut to fit saucepan to retain moisture). Strain, remove the bay leaves and mash the ingredients to a paste by pushing through a drum sieve (commonly used to create smooth sauces). Add the olive oil and tahini and season to taste.

MIXED BEANS
1/2 cup borlotti beans
1/2 cup red kidney beans
1/2 cup white kidney beans
5 cloves garlic, peeled
1/2 brown onion, peeled and finely sliced
150ml white wine
150ml water
150ml olive oil
1 bay leaf

Soak the beans overnight and cook separately as each type will have a different cooking time. Combine all the ingredients and simmer, covered with a cartouche, until tender. Repeat with fresh ingredients for the other two types of beans. Separate the beans from the cooked ingredients before serving.

MUSTARD EMULSION
100g Dijon mustard
50ml white balsamic vinegar
3 tablespoons Keens mustard powder
200ml olive oil
juice of 1 lemon

Mix all the ingredients together.

GREEN SOYBEANS WITH PORT BUTTER
100ml port
30g butter, diced
1/2 cup soybeans

Flambé the port and stir in the butter to thicken. While hot, mix in the soybeans and set aside.

TOASTED DESICCATED COCONUT
100g desiccated coconut
2 teaspoons ground turmeric
3 drops lemon juice

Combine all the ingredients and dry-roast in a heavy-based pan until fragrant.

To finish and serve
freshly chopped tomato
finely minced parsley

Spoon some broad bean purée on each plate, top with an eggplant timbale and spoon some mustard emulsion over. Arrange the beans around the plates and garnish with zucchini chips and desiccated coconut. Garnish with tomato and parsley.

Serves 6

Recipe from Cheong Liew
GRANGE RESTAURANT
HILTON ADELAIDE HOTEL
ADELAIDE

Recommended wine:
Alan and Veitch Adelaide Hills
Viognier 2005

ADELAIDE ARCADE
ADELAIDE
ARCADE
115
CLARKE
GOLD SHOP
SALE

Seared Miso-crusted Wagyu Beef

with grilled mushroom salad and Japanese mustard sauce

MISO BASE
100ml mirin
150g white miso
70g caster sugar

600g wagyu beef (sirloin)

Flambé the mirin in a hot pan over a low heat. Add the miso and sugar and stir until dissolved. Remove from the heat and cool, then brush all over the beef.

LEFT: This ornate tiled fountain is located outside the historic Adelaide Arcade off Rundle Mall in the heart of the city.

Preheat the oven to 180°C. In a hot pan sear the steaks until a nice crust forms on all sides, then roast for 3–4 minutes. Remove from the oven and rest for 8–10 minutes.

JAPANESE MUSTARD SAUCE
1/4 cup cooked baby spinach
1/2 cup miso base (remaining from above)
60ml chicken stock
1 teaspoon Japanese mustard powder
60ml rice wine vinegar

With a hand blender purée the spinach, miso and chicken stock to a fine paste. Add the mustard powder and vinegar to taste.

MUSHROOM SALAD
1/2 cup enoki mushrooms
1/2 cup shimeji mushrooms
1/2 cup chestnut mushrooms
1/2 cup shiitake mushrooms
olive oil for frying
1 tablespoon sesame seeds, toasted
25ml Japanese soy sauce
1 cup mizuna leaves

Clean and quarter the mushrooms and sauté in hot olive oil until just cooked. Add the sesame seeds, soy sauce and mizuna leaves.

To serve
Spread a thin bed of sauce over each plate. Slice the beef thinly across the grain and place on the sauce. Top with some mushroom salad.

Serves 6

Recipe from Tony Carroll
JOLLEYS BOATHOUSE
ADELAIDE

Recommended wine:
Ceravolo Adelaide Plains
Sangiovese 2004

Crisp Tunisian Duck Brik

with harissa, date, blood orange and watercress salad

4 x 180g duck legs
200ml olive oil
2 teaspoons cumin seeds
1 teaspoon coriander seeds
1 teaspoon fennel seeds
salt
zest from 1 orange
3 sheets brik pastry, halved
60g melted butter

SALAD
8 Medjool dates, peeled, pitted and sliced
1 orange, cut into segments (reserve the juice)
20g pistachio nuts
1/4 cup coriander leaves
1/4 cup mint leaves
1 cup watercress, picked over

Preheat the oven to 140°C. Season the duck legs and seal in a hot pan with the olive oil until golden brown. Place in the oven for 40–50 minutes.

Roast, grind and sieve the spices.

Remove the duck from the oven and allow to cool slightly, then discard the skin, bones and any gristle. Shred the meat and season with the spices, salt and the orange zest.

Press the duck mixture into a dish lined with greaseproof paper, cover with more greaseproof and place a heavy object on top. Refrigerate overnight.

Turn the pressed duck out onto a chopping board, remove the greaseproof paper and cut into 6 equal portions.

Brush the pastry sheets with butter, place a duck portion on a sheet of pastry and roll over, tucking in ends until completely wrapped. With a sharp knife trim off any excess pastry. Repeat with the remaining portions. Brush the tops with more butter. Refrigerate until ready to serve, then bake at 200°C for 12 minutes or until the pastry is crisp.

To serve
2 tablespoons harissa
extra virgin olive oil
pomegranate molasses (available at Middle Eastern food stores)

Smear each plate lightly with harissa and place the duck brik on top. Mix together all the salad ingredients with the reserved orange juice and place alongside the brik. Drizzle the plate with extra virgin olive oil and pomegranate molasses.

NOTE: Brik pastry is a Tunisian wheat-based pastry, similar to filo, available at Middle Eastern food stores.

Serves 6

Recipe from Tony Carroll
JOLLEYS BOATHOUSE
ADELAIDE

Recommended wine:
Grant Burge Barossa Valley Benchmark Unoaked Chardonnay 2005

BELOW: *Fractal Mandala* in steel sheet by Greg Johns was commissioned by the South Australian Government for the Torrens Riverbank.

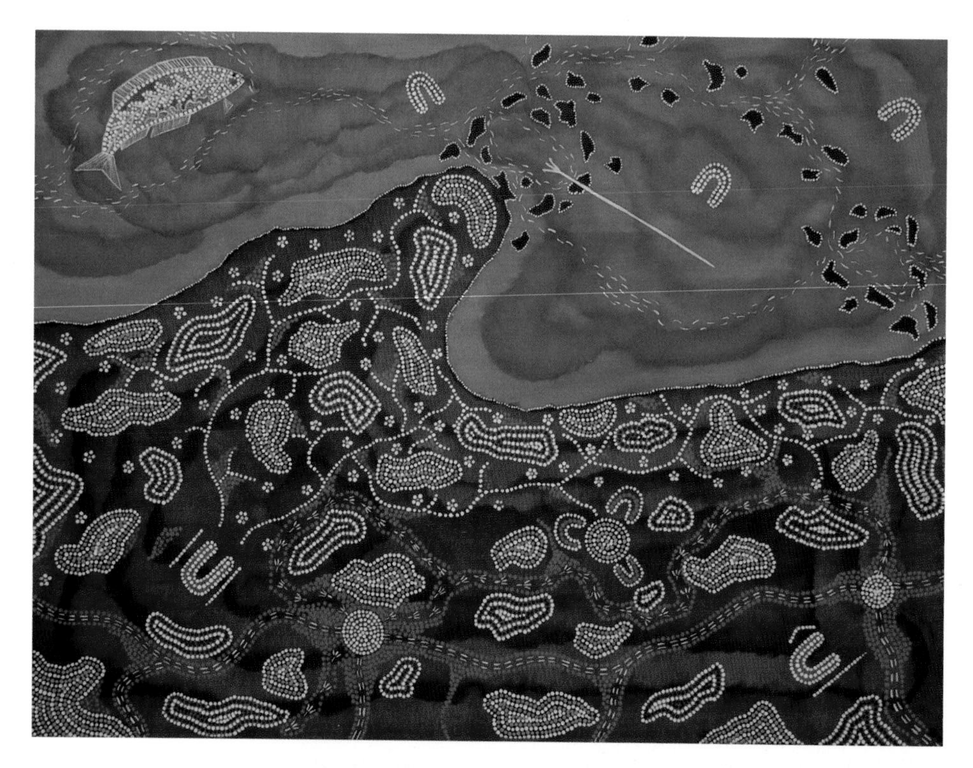

ABOVE AND RIGHT: Two works in acrylic on canvas by young Aboriginal artist Joseph Cattermole. ABOVE: *Cycle of Life* depicts hunting and gathering trails within the coastal fringes of Adjahdura lands. RIGHT: *Adjahdura Oolta (Land of My Country).*

RIGHT: Glenelg is a popular beach-side suburb of Adelaide located on the shore of Holdfast Bay in Gulf Saint Vincent. It is the oldest European settlement on mainland South Australia.

POLITE
Pas

ABOVE: Piles of mine tailings at Coober Pedy, known as the opal capital of the world and also famous for its unique style of underground living.

Spinach Gnocchi

250g gnocchi
6 leaves spinach, destemmed
30ml olive oil plus extra for drizzling
4 cups chopped mushrooms
1 clove garlic, peeled and chopped
6 semi-dried tomatoes
30ml white wine
6 leaves basil, chopped
pinch each of salt and freshly ground black pepper
½ teaspoon chilli flakes (optional)
1 teaspoon chopped parsley

Place the gnocchi in a saucepan of boiling, salted water. As the gnocchi start to float (about 6 minutes), add the spinach leaves. Continue to cook for 2 minutes, or until the gnocchi are fully floating. Drain.

Place the olive oil in a heated frying pan and sauté the mushrooms. Add the garlic, semi-dried tomatoes and white wine. Mix well.

Add the gnocchi and spinach leaves to the pan. Sauté the mixture then add the basil, salt and pepper, and chilli if using.

Serve garnished with chopped parsley and top with a drizzle of olive oil.

Serves 1

Recipe from Adriana Lombardi
CAPRICCIO
GLENELG

Recommended wine:
Bent Creek Adelaide Hills
Sauvignon Blanc 2005

RIGHT: A pendant in solid sterling silver and gold, inset with opals and made by master goldsmith and designing goldsmith partnership Volker and Marianne Sprinkmeier.

Naturally beautiful
TASMANIA
JRC

WIDELY PRAISED FOR ITS WILDERNESS areas that include 17 national parks, Australia's island state is a favourite destination for nature lovers from around the world.

The region claims to have the world's cleanest air and purest water – hard to prove, but it is certainly true that many of the beaches are near-deserted and the lakes are as clear as crystal.

The spectacular scenery has ecology groups constantly on the alert for rapacious developers. Visitors to any of the island's towns or cities should be prepared to sign a petition or two.

The natural beauty also acts as inspiration for local artists and craftspeople. Every town, no matter how small, seems to boast at least one craft shop or art gallery, and the number is multiplied considerably in the two major cities, Launceston and Hobart.

The performing arts are held in equally high esteem, as is well demonstrated by the crowds who queue for shows at Hobart's meticulously maintained Theatre Royal, built in 1837.

Astute chefs make good use of local specialties, many of them seldom seen away from the island. Their dishes are partnered by wine that is quite different from that made in other parts of the country, thanks to the relatively cool climate.

Under its former name, Van Diemen's Land, Tasmania was heavily involved in the development of Australia as a penal colony, an aspect of local history in which today's residents take a perverse pride. Several museums pay tribute to these forced pioneers, many of whom rose above their harsh arrival and went on to make major contributions to society.

It is called the Island State – singular – but Tasmania is separated from the mainland by an archipelago of more than 300 smaller islands, some of which can be visited. By any measure, this is an extraordinary part of Australia.

LEFT: The 1271m-high Mt Wellington towers over the boat harbour of Hobart.

Slow-cooked Pork Belly

with Spring Bay scallops

CHINESE MASTER STOCK

500ml water
100g (about 1/2 cup) yellow rock sugar (available from Asian food stores)
3 star anise
250ml light soy sauce
1 slice fresh ginger
150ml dark soy sauce
1 piece dry mandarin peel
250ml Chinese rice cooking wine
1/2 quill cinnamon
1/2 teaspoon coriander seeds
1 teaspoon whole Szechuan peppercorns
1 dried long chilli
1/2 teaspoon fennel seeds
pinch of dried chilli flakes

Bring the water to the boil, then add the sugar and dissolve. Add the remaining ingredients and simmer for 1 hour. Cool overnight. Strain before use.

PORK BELLY

1/2 side pork belly, about 1kg, preferably top end with bone in

Preheat the oven to 170°C. With a blowtorch burn any hairs from the pork skin. Place skin-side down in a roasting dish with the Chinese master stock, cover and place in the oven for 1 1/2 hours. Remove from the oven, turn over carefully and cook for another 1 1/2 hours.

Remove from the oven, cool to handling temperature, then take out of the liquid. Carefully remove the rib bones and cartilage from the underside. Place the pork in a dish between 2 sheets of baking paper, place a weight on top and refrigerate overnight.

The following day, trim the sides down and cut into 8 entrée or 4 main portions.

SPICY PLUM SAUCE

1 knob ginger, grated
2 cloves garlic, peeled and chopped
500ml plum sauce
100ml sweet chilli sauce
50ml light soy sauce
1 bunch coriander, chopped

Place all the ingredients except the coriander in a small saucepan and simmer for 15 minutes. Cool, then add the coriander.

To finish and serve

36 good-sized Spring Bay scallops
100ml olive oil
salt and freshly ground black pepper
fried shallots (available from Asian food stores)
1 bunch fresh coriander, chopped

Preheat the oven to 180°C. Shallow-fry the pork belly on all sides until crisp. Transfer to the oven and bake for 10 minutes.

With a sharp knife remove the membrane from the scallops. Coat with olive oil and season with salt and pepper. Heat a steel or cast-iron pan and, when very hot, spread the oiled scallops in the dry pan, and cook for 30 seconds on each side.

Drizzle the plates with a little plum sauce. Cut each piece of pork in half lengthwise, and arrange centrally crossed over each other. Arrange scallops around the outside and garnish with fried shallots and coriander.

Serves 8 as an entrée or 4 as a main

Recipe from Danny Roberts
BLUE SKIES CAFÉ
RESTAURANT & BAR
HOBART

Recommended wine:
South Pirie Pinot Noir 2005

Salmon Nori Rolls

with wasabi-dressed salad and sweet chilli sauce

8 x 100g large batons cut from 1 whole side of salmon, skinned and pin bones removed
8 nori sheets

Brush a nori sheet lightly with water on both sides. Wrap each salmon baton in a nori sheet from corner to corner, folding outer corners in. This is best done a couple of hours in advance as the nori sheet will shrink around the salmon.

SWEET CHILLI SAUCE
350g white sugar
100g brown sugar
150g grated palm sugar
200ml fresh squeezed lime juice
600ml water
1 tablespoon chopped garlic
2 teaspoons chopped fresh bird's eye chillies (or jalapeño as milder option)
3 tablespoons chopped parsley
3 tablespoons chopped coriander

Place the sugars in a 3-litre saucepan. Add the lime juice and water, then bring to the boil and reduce by half. Brush the sides of the saucepan occasionally with a wet pastry brush to avoid crystallising the syrup.

Remove from the heat and add the garlic and chillies. Stir to infuse the flavours. After a few minutes add the herbs but not when the syrup is still too hot or they will lose their colour. Bring to room temperature and shake well before serving.

SALAD
1 tube wasabi paste
100ml plain mayonnaise (preferably homemade)
1 red capsicum, julienned
100g pea shoots, halved
100g bean shoots
100g leek, thinly sliced
1 bunch Thai basil leaves (reserve 4 tips to garnish)
1 bunch Vietnamese mint leaves (reserve 4 tips to garnish)
1 cucumber (not bitter), peeled into ribbons
100g crushed roasted peanuts

Mix together the wasabi and mayonnaise to the desired strength. Combine the salad ingredients and dress with the wasabi mayonnaise.

TEMPURA BATTER
350g plain flour
50g cornflour
1 tablespoon salt
750ml soda water
handful ice cubes

Place all the flour and the salt in a large bowl and pour in the soda water. Whisk lightly together. Add the ice cubes.

To finish and serve
oil for deep-frying
1 bunch bok choy, washed and quartered
50g fried shallots (available from Asian food stores)

Dip the nori rolls in the tempura batter to coat them lightly. If using a small fryer, deep-fry at 180°C for 3 ½ minutes. If using a large saucepan, fry 2 at a time for 2 ½ minutes, transferring to an oven tray until all are done. Place in a hot oven for 2 minutes. Repeat the process with the bok choy.

Halve the salmon packages diagonally and arrange on plates with the salad. Garnish with the reserved mint and basil tips and sprinkle with crisp fried shallots. Drizzle a little sweet chilli sauce around the plates.

NOTE: Any leftover Sweet Chilli Sauce will keep well if refrigerated.

Serves 4

Recipe from Danny Roberts
BLUE SKIES CAFÉ
RESTAURANT & BAR
HOBART

Recommended wine:
Bream Creek Chardonnay 2004

LEFT: *Rainforest Tasmania* is a low-fired ceramic bowl with a copper glaze by Jude Sercombe.

Organic Market Salad

VINAIGRETTE

1/2 cup extra virgin olive oil
1/2 cup white wine vinegar
2 tablespoons Dijon mustard
salt and freshly ground black pepper

Whisk together all the ingredients.

SALAD

2 large free-range chicken breasts
olive oil for rubbing
salt and freshly ground black pepper
2 tangelos (can substitute blood oranges or mandarins)
1 bunch watercress or rocket, stems discarded
2 ripe avocados, peeled and sliced

Preheat the oven to 180°C. Rub the chicken with olive oil, then season. Cook slowly in the oven until cooked through but still tender. Slice and set aside.

Peel the tangelos with a paring knife, taking care to remove the pith, and slice into rounds.

Place the watercress in a large bowl with the avocado, tangelo and sliced chicken. Add some of the vinaigrette and carefully toss with your hands to coat ingredients.

To serve
Arrange on white plates to show off the colours.

Serves 4 as a light lunch

Recipe from Megan Quill
TRICYCLE CAFÉ BAR
SALAMANCA
HOBART

Recommended wine:
Lalla Gully Riesling 2005

RIGHT: The Tasmanian Wilderness World Heritage Area is one of the largest conservation reserves in Australia, covering about 20 percent of the land area of the island.

Breakfast Trifle

1kg rhubarb (preferably organic), leaves and green bits discarded, chopped into 2cm lengths
1 vanilla bean
1/2 cup caster sugar
30–50ml water
3/4 cup rolled oats
1/8 cup rolled rye
1/8 cup rolled barley
1 cup creamy Greek-style yoghurt
1 tablespoon slivered almonds to garnish

Place the rhubarb in a saucepan with the vanilla bean, sugar and water. Simmer gently over a low heat until the rhubarb is tender and starting to break up. Taste for sweetness and add more sugar if desired. Split the vanilla bean and scrape the fragrant black paste into the fruit. Stir well to distribute vanilla and break up the rhubarb (it should be sloppy).

Mix the grains together.

Place layers of the yoghurt, grains and rhubarb, in that order, into a tall glass, spooning in a little of the poaching liquid with the fruit to moisten the grains. Finish with a good dollop of yoghurt and a sprinkling of almonds.

NOTE: Apple purée or slow-poached quince can be used instead of rhubarb.

This recipe will make more rhubarb than you'll need. Reserve the rest for another dish.

Serves 1

Recipe from Megan Quill
TRICYCLE
SALAMANCA
HOBART

Recommended wine:

Pipers Brook Ninth Island
Sparkling NV

LEFT: *All That You Bring* is an oil on Belgian linen work by Luke Wagner.

BELOW: *Dancing in the Flow* is an oil on canvas work by Catherine Stringer. It is one of a series of underwater figures which explore the deeper aspects of human experience.

Cosmopolitan melting pot

VICTORIA

VICTORIA COULD WELL LAY CLAIM to being Australia's most cosmopolitan state. Wander around Melbourne and your senses will be put on high alert. The inviting aromas of great coffee might fill the air on one corner. Stroll a bit further and you will be tempted by Chinese-spiced chickens and ducks being barbecued over an open flame. Curry might star in another street, or perhaps Thai or Vietnamese scents such as lemongrass and galangal, a relation of ginger.

The aromatic impressions are concentrated in the city's markets. These colourful 'must-visit' destinations for enthusiastic foodies offer a huge range of produce from suppliers around the state and other parts of Australia, as well as hard-to-find imported ingredients.

Where there are great markets and food stores, there must be great cafés and restaurants. Landmark establishments include The Flower Drum, which has been called the greatest Chinese restaurant in the world, France-Soir, a faithful recreation of a Paris bistro, and the Italian Grossi Florentino, but these old hands are joined weekly, or so it seems, by enthusiastic newcomers.

The city's passion for fine food and wine is echoed around the state. Mornington Peninsula, about an hour's drive from Melbourne, not only has appealing beaches, but also a great range of wineries, cafés and restaurants.

The Yarra Valley was the first region to alert the world to Victoria's suitability for the grape, but excellent wines are made in other parts of the state. Shiraz performs well on the right site and in Rutherglen, near where bushranger Ned Kelly met his demise, a unique fortified Muscat is produced. Honeyed, rich and delicious, it regularly receives rave reviews from international pundits.

Art has always played an important in the Victorian lifestyle. Melbourne's National Gallery of Victoria, which opened its doors in 1861, was recently split into two buildings, one for Australian art, the other for international pieces. Both are well worth a visit.

LEFT: Known as the Twelve Apostles, this collection of natural limestone stacks stands just offshore in the Port Campbell National Park. The ocean's powerful forces have eroded their bases and now only eight remain.

Westernport Rock Flathead

with fennel cream sauce and homemade linguini

4 x 160g fresh skinned rock flathead tail fillets
knob of butter
fresh herbs such as thyme, oregano, parsley

Rub the fish with butter and fresh herbs and wrap it loosely in greaseproof paper. Refrigerate until needed.

FENNEL CREAM SAUCE
olive oil for frying
2 bulbs fennel, diced into 1cm cubes
2 stalks celery, diced into1cm cubes
1 clove garlic, peeled and crushed
1 teaspoon fennel seeds
200ml white wine
500ml fish stock
1 tablespoon Pernod
200ml cream

In a saucepan heat a small amount of olive oil and sauté the fennel and celery. After a few minutes add the garlic and fennel seeds, sauté for a further 5 minutes, then reduce the heat and cover. Cook for 10 minutes, then add the wine, stock, Pernod and cream, and simmer for 10 minutes. Purée in a blender until smooth. Pass through a fine sieve. Set aside.

PASTA
200g high-grade flour
300g semolina flour
5 whole eggs
2 egg yolks
2 teaspoons olive oil

Place both flours in a mound on a bench and make a well in the centre. Beat together the eggs and yolks and pour into the well along with the oil. Gradually combine together to form a smooth dough. Wrap in plastic cling film and refrigerate for 1 hour. Roll the dough through a pasta machine to the second setting, then cut into 1cm strips (using the machine attachment or by hand).

To finish and serve
sea salt to season
ground star anise to season
1 tablespoon dried pink peppercorns
2 stalks dill, chopped, plus extra sprigs to garnish
olive oil

Preheat the oven to 180°C. Season the fish and bake until cooked through but still moist (8 minutes). Warm the sauce in a saucepan, season with sea salt, star anise and pink peppercorns, and add the dill.
Cook the pasta in boiling, salted water until al dente. Drain, toss in olive oil then roll portions on a fork and place in serving bowls. Top with the fish and spoon the sauce over. Drizzle with olive oil and garnish with dill sprigs.

Serves 4

Recipe from Barry Davis
MONTALTO VINEYARD
AND OLIVE GROVE
MORNINGTON PENINSULA

Recommended wine:
Montalto Mornington Peninsula
Pennon Hill Rosé 2005

RIGHT: *Lux*, an etched and sandblasted blown glass vase by Tony Hanning.

Confit Pork Belly

with spiced apple and potato purée

1kg pork belly
$^2/_3$ cup coarse sea salt
1kg duck fat, melted
2 tablespoons white peppercorns

Place the pork skin-side down on a dish, salt the meat and refrigerate for 24 hours.

Preheat the oven to 140°C. Rub off the salt, then place the pork in a large, deep roasting dish. Cover with duck fat and sprinkle with peppercorns. Cook for 3 hours or until tender. Remove from the duck fat, cool and cut into 4 squares.

SPICED APPLE
2 Granny Smith apples, peeled, cored and halved
50g unsalted butter
2 teaspoons liquid honey
pinch of nutmeg
pinch of mace
pinch of ground ginger
1 cardamom pod
pinch of ground white pepper
1 cinnamon quill

Place the apples, cut-side down, and the butter in a hot pan over a medium heat. Mix together the honey and spices, and pour over the apples. Keep moving the apples around in the pan until they are caramelised and cooked.

500g Royal Blue potatoes, peeled and halved
200g butter
salt and nutmeg to season

Boil the potatoes in salted water until tender. Drain and mash, then mix through the butter, and add salt and nutmeg to taste.

To finish and serve
sprig of rosemary to garnish

Roast the pork squares in a preheated 180°C oven for 10 minutes.

To serve, place a quenelle of potato in the centre of each plate, place the apple on top and the pork to the side. Drizzle with jus from the pork.

Serves 4

Recipe from Barry Davis
MONTALTO VINEYARD
AND OLIVE GROVE
MORNINGTON PENINSULA

Recommended wine:
Montalto Mornington Peninsula
Pinot Noir 2005

ABOVE: *Coil*, a silicon bronze sculpture by Andrew Rogers.

OUT OF ORDER
LADIES
OUT OF ORDER
GENTS

ABOVE: The rolling vineyards of Montalto Estate, Mornington Peninsula.

LEFT: The work of local mural artists on public toilets spotted on the Great Ocean Road.

RIGHT: The town of Clunes was home to Victoria's first registered gold strike on 7 July 1851 and retains many of the elegant historic buildings from that time.

BOTTOM RIGHT: Advertising sign for ice cream on a roadside fence, southern Victoria.

ABOVE: The Great Ocean Road hugs the coastline along the entire length of the Port Campbell National Park, known for its amazing collection of rock sculptures.

Artichoke and Tonka Bean Soup

with dehydrated bacon

ARTICHOKE SOUP

3 onions, peeled and diced
oil for frying
2kg Jerusalem artichokes, peeled and chopped
15 tonka beans (substitute 1 vanilla bean if unavailable)
1 litre chicken stock
500ml milk
300ml cream
salt and pepper to taste

Sweat the onions in a little oil. Add the artichokes and fry for 5 minutes. Add the tonka beans and stock, bring to the boil and simmer for 20 minutes. Add the milk and cream and bring back to the boil. Purée in a blender until smooth, then season.

ROASTED ARTICHOKE PURÉE

500g Jerusalem artichokes, peeled and chopped
oil for frying
1 sprig thyme
1 clove garlic

Preheat the oven to 160°C. Fry the artichokes in a pan with a little oil until golden. Place in a roasting tray with the garlic and thyme then cook for 20 minutes. Purée in a blender until smooth.

To finish and serve
dehydrated bacon

Warm the purée and soup. Place 1 spoonful of purée each in the base of 8 soup bowls, then spoon the soup in. Garnish with crisp bacon, or serve as in photograph.

Serves 8

Recipe from Robin Wickens
INTERLUDE
MELBOURNE

Recommended wine:
YarraLoch Yarra Valley Arneis 2005

ABOVE AND LEFT: *What a Whopper* and *Uncle Jack Catching Yabbies* are two of a series of paintings by Bob Marchant which recapture some of his childhood memories of yabbie-catching expeditions.

Crisp Red Mullet

with bouillabaisse and rouille

BOUILLABAISSE

1 carrot, scrubbed and chopped
1 onion, peeled and chopped
1 stick celery, chopped
1 leek, chopped
1 head garlic, peeled and chopped
oil for frying
2 tablespoons tomato paste
200ml Noilly Pratt (or other dry vermouth)
4 crayfish heads and shells
1.5 litres fish stock
1 tablespoon black peppercorns
1 tablespoon coriander seeds
3 star anise
2 sprigs thyme
pinch of saffron
salt and freshly ground black pepper

Preheat the oven to 220°C. Sweat the vegetables in a little oil until caramelised. Add the tomato paste and deglaze the pan with the vermouth.

Roast the crayfish shells for 20 minutes, then place in a large saucepan with the remaining ingredients, except the saffron. Bring to the boil, skimming constantly. Add the saffron and simmer for 35 minutes. Strain the stock then reduce by half. Season to taste.

ROUILLE

4 tablespoons mashed potato
1 hard-boiled egg yolk
2 egg yolks
1 tablespoon chopped and deseeded chilli
2 cloves garlic, peeled
pinch of saffron, soaked in 50ml warm water
250ml light olive oil
salt and freshly ground black pepper
juice of 1 lemon

Combine the potato with the yolks, chilli, garlic and saffron in a food processor. Add the oil in a thin stream until the mixture thickens (as for making mayonnaise). Season and add lemon juice to taste.

To finish and serve

olive oil for frying
8 fillets red mullet, skin on
1 potato, peeled and finely diced

Heat some oil in a non-stick pan. Fry the mullet skin-side down for 3 minutes until crisp and golden. Turn over and cook for a further 30 seconds. Drain on kitchen paper.

In a saucepan, add olive oil to a depth of 1cm and heat until very hot. Add the diced potato, stirring constantly until crisp and golden.

Spoon the thick bouillabaisse into serving bowls. Top each with a red mullet fillet, some rouille and fried potato.

Serves 8

Recipe from Robin Wickens
INTERLUDE
MELBOURNE

Recommended wine:
Sorrenberg Beechworth
Sauvignon Blanc/Semillon 2005

Strawberry and Rose Petal Pavlova

with pistachio praline

250g (about 8) egg whites
375g sugar
1/2 teaspoon vanilla
2 teaspoons cornflour
2 teaspoons white vinegar
400ml thickened cream
1 tablespoon icing sugar
1/2 teaspoon vanilla paste (or extract)

Preheat the oven to 160°C. Line a Swiss roll tin with greaseproof paper.

Beat the egg whites until stiff, then gradually beat in the sugar until the whites are thick and glossy. Fold in the vanilla, cornflour and vinegar. Spread mixture into the prepared tin. Bake for 20 minutes.

Remove from the oven and allow to cool for a few minutes, then turn out onto a sheet of greaseproof paper dusted with icing sugar. Allow to cool for a further 10 minutes.

Whip the cream in a chilled bowl until firm peaks form, then fold in the icing sugar and vanilla. Spread the vanilla cream over the meringue and roll carefully using the baking paper to keep it firm. Wrap in plastic cling film and refrigerate on a tray for 3 hours before serving.

ROSE PETAL SYRUP (OPTIONAL)

4 cups water
2 cups sugar
1 stick cinnamon
2 tablespoons lemon juice
2 tablespoons rose water

Bring the water, sugar and cinnamon to the boil, then simmer for 5 minutes. Allow to cool and remove the cinnamon.

When the syrup is cold add the lemon juice and rose water.

PISTACHIO PRALINE

1/4 cup caster sugar
1/4 cup water
1/4 cup pistachios, shelled

Heat the sugar and water until medium brown. Add the pistachios and stir through. Pour onto a greased baking tray and allow to cool.

To serve

fresh strawberries
fresh rose petals (or dried rose petals, available from specialty shops)

Cut the pavlova roulade into rounds. Serve garnished with strawberries, rose petals and broken pieces of the praline. Drizzle with rose petal syrup if desired.

Serves 6–8

Recipe from Cath Claringbold
MECCA RESTAURANT
MELBOURNE

Recommended wine:

Stella Bella Margaret River
Pink Muscat 2005

Seared Scallops on Skordalia

with sauce vierge

SKORDALIA
1kg Desiree potatoes
20ml vinegar
100ml olive oil
2 tablespoons crushed garlic
½ teaspoon salt

Boil the potatoes in salted water until tender, then mash until smooth. Add the vinegar, olive oil and garlic, mix well, and add salt.

SAUCE VIERGE
3 tomatoes, peeled, deseeded and diced
50ml olive oil
50ml lemon juice
5 leaves basil, washed and finely sliced
1 teaspoon coriander seeds, roasted and crushed
pinch of salt

Place all the ingredients in a small saucepan and just warm. Do not boil.

To finish and serve
16 Canadian scallops
oil for frying

Heat a pan with a little oil and sear the scallops on both sides until golden brown.

Put the skordalia in a piping bag and pipe 4 mounds the size of the scallops onto each of 4 plates. Top each mound with a scallop, then drizzle a spoonful of sauce over.

Serves 4

Recipe from John Psanis
QUAFF RESTAURANT
MELBOURNE

Recommended wine:
Kiltynane Estate Preliminaire
Tarrawarra Blanc de Noir 2005

ABOVE: Sunlight enhances the dome of Melbourne's historic Flinders Street Station.

Swap the remote for the remote.
TASMANIA

Crisp Duck Confit

with parmesan polenta and Madeira sage jus

DUCK CONFIT

50g sea salt
4 duck legs
2 sprigs thyme
2 bay leaves
500ml duck fat or canola oil

Salt the duck legs, add the bay leaves and thyme, and refrigerate overnight. When ready to confit, brush off the excess salt and herbs. Bring the fat or oil to the boil, reduce to a simmer, then add the duck legs, skin-side up. Cook for 2–2 ½ hours until tender. Remove and cool. Reserve fat.

MADEIRA SAGE JUS

100ml Madeira
300ml chicken stock, reduced
15 sprigs sage
salt and freshly ground black pepper

Simmer the Madeira until reduced by half. Add the stock and simmer for a further 5 minutes.

Take off the heat, add the sage and allow to infuse for about 1 hour. Strain and season.

PARMESAN POLENTA

800ml milk
2 cloves garlic, peeled and crushed
200g instant polenta
50g parmesan, grated

Place the milk and garlic in a saucepan and bring to the boil. Add the polenta and cook according to the instructions on the packet, stirring continuously until thickened to the consistency of mashed potato. Add the parmesan and continue to stir until fully cooked. Cover and leave in a warm place.

To finish and serve

Preheat the oven to 180°C. Heat oil or duck fat reserved from the confit in a roasting dish and add the duck legs skin-side down. Roast for 5–15 minutes until crisp. Divide the polenta among 4 bowls and place a duck leg on each serving. Pour the jus over, topping each leg with sage leaves.

Serves 4

Recipe from Petar Mardesic
PUNCH LANE WINE BAR AND RESTAURANT
MELBOURNE

Recommended wine:
Curlewis Pinot Noir 2003

ABOVE: Point Nepean is a highlight of the Mornington Peninsula National Park and provides panoramic views of Bass Strait.

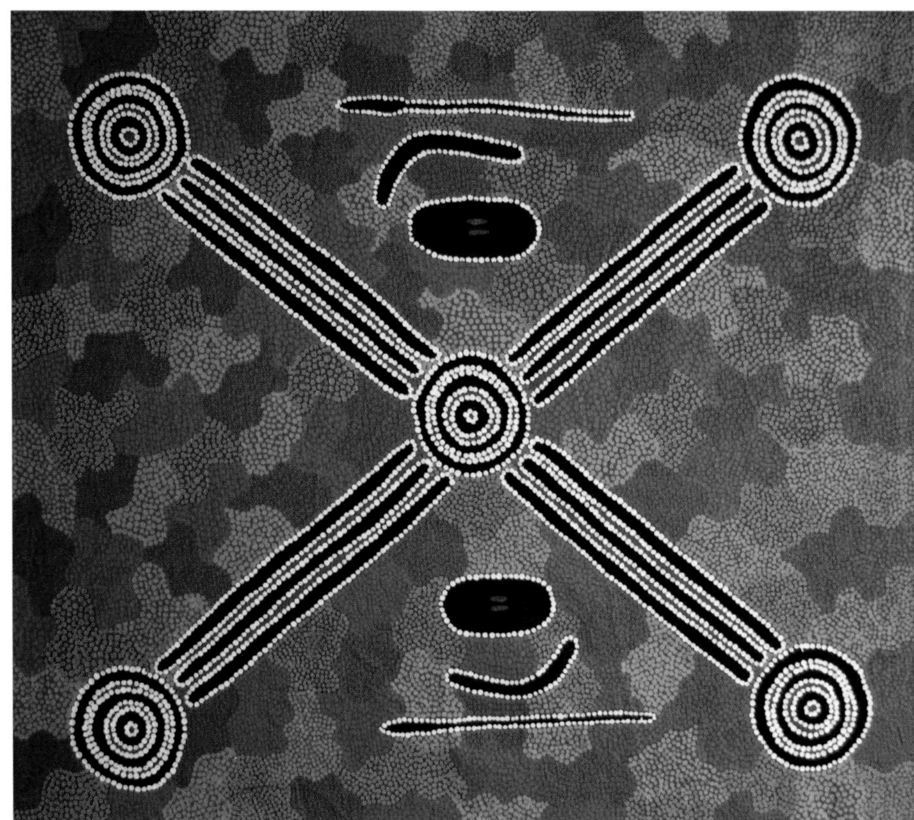

ABOVE: Hanging in the Lancefield Gallery, this traditional design using acrylic on board is by Jimmy Warrinya.

Sautéed Field Mushrooms and Chorizo Sausage

with parsley in a sherry sauce

2 chorizo sausages, skinned and sliced
1 tablespoon olive oil
4 field mushrooms, roasted and cut into 8 pieces
1 clove garlic, peeled and chopped
80ml sherry vinegar
1 tablespoon chopped parsley
40g butter
salt and freshly ground black pepper

Sauté the chorizo in olive oil on medium heat until the paprika leaches out. Add the mushrooms and garlic, and cook for a further 2 minutes. Add the sherry vinegar. When it starts to bubble, add the butter. Stir through, then add parsley and seasoning.

Serves 4

Recipe from Petar Mardesic
PUNCH LANE WINE BAR AND RESTAURANT
MELBOURNE

Recommended wine:
Ashton Hills Vineyard Three Pinot Gris Riesling 2004

MARTINI
AND THE BONE PALACE ORCHESTRA
Debut Album Launch
DREAM UNTIL YOU
July 29th @THE SPANISH CLUB 59-61
with

ABOVE: An ornately decorated lamp post in the centre of Melbourne.

RIGHT: Origami cranes, made by school children and symbolising world peace, hang in the Melbourne City Art Gallery.

FAR RIGHT: A colourful poster brightens up a city power pole.

ABOVE: The Southbank promenade along the Yarra River is one of Melbourne's most popular dining areas with its riverside setting and views of the city skyline.

Spiced Lamb Tagine

with preserved lemon and green olives

mild olive oil
3 sticks celery, diced small
2 carrots, scrubbed and diced small
2 medium onions, peeled and finely diced
6 cloves garlic, peeled and finely chopped
1 tablespoon cumin seeds
1 tablespoon coriander seeds
1/4 teaspoon ground turmeric
1/4 teaspoon ground ginger
1/4 teaspoon ground cinnamon
pinch of saffron
1 boned lamb shoulder (1.5–2kg), cut into 6cm pieces
2 x 400g cans chopped Italian tomatoes
2 bay leaves
2 sprigs thyme
2–3 litres chicken stock or water
2 tablespoons honey
2 tablespoons harissa, or to taste
1 cup pitted green olives, halved
1 tablespoon finely sliced preserved lemon
salt and freshly ground black pepper
1 cup coriander leaves
1 cup parsley leaves
steamed couscous to serve

In a pan large enough to hold the lamb, heat a good splash of olive oil, add the vegetables and garlic and cook over a low heat for 15–20 minutes or until completely soft, but not brown.

In a dry frying pan gently toast the cumin and coriander seeds just until fragrant, then crush finely with a mortar and pestle. Mix with the other spices and add to the vegetables.

Increase the heat to medium and stir for 2 minutes, then add the lamb, tomatoes, bay leaves, thyme and enough stock or water to cover. Bring to the boil, skim any fat from the surface, then reduce the heat to low and simmer very gently for 2 hours or until the meat is very tender.

Skim any remaining fat from the surface, then add the honey, harissa, olives and preserved lemon. Season to taste, then transfer to a tagine dish for serving.

Generously scatter with the herbs and serve immediately with steamed couscous.

Serves 8

Recipe from Cath Claringbold
MECCA RESTAURANT
MELBOURNE

Recommended wine:

John Duval Barossa Valley Plexus Shiraz/Grenache Mourvèdre 2004

ABOVE: Colourful bathing boxes, remnants of a Victorian past, decorate the beaches of Mornington Peninsula.

Roasted Lamb Rump Stack

with feta, eggplant and Madeira sauce

BASIL PESTO

1 bunch basil, washed and leaves picked
50g pine nuts
100g parmesan
200ml olive oil
2 cloves garlic, peeled and crushed
salt and freshly ground black pepper

Place all the ingredients in a food processor and blend to a fine purée, then season with salt and pepper.

MADEIRA SAUCE

500ml lamb stock
50ml Madeira
20g butter

Simmer the lamb stock to reduce by half. Add the Madeira and stir in the butter.

LAMB

2 lamb rumps, trimmed
oil for frying

Preheat the oven to 180°C. Seal the lamb in a little oil in a hot pan until golden brown, then place in the oven for about 10 minutes. When cooked, allow to rest before slicing.

To finish and serve

4 x 1cm-thick slices eggplant
olive oil for frying
120g Bulgarian feta, sliced

Pan-fry the eggplant slices in oil until golden brown and tender. Place 1 slice in a bowl, then arrange sliced feta to cover. Top with sliced lamb. Spread a thin layer of basil pesto on a second eggplant slice and place on top. Repeat for second serving. Drizzle the Madeira sauce around the stack.

Serves 2

Recipe from John Psanis
QUAFF RESTAURANT
MELBOURNE

Recommended wine:

Casa Freschi La Signora
Langhorne Creek 2002

Seared Scallops and White-cut Chicken

with sweet corn custard and pickled mushrooms

WHITE-CUT CHICKEN

1 free-range chicken
5 litres light chicken stock
2cm piece fresh ginger
2 spring onions (white only), chopped
1 teaspoon sugar

Remove the legs from the chicken and reserve for another use. Bring the stock, ginger, spring onions and sugar to the boil.

Drop the chicken into the stock and bring back to the boil. Reduce the heat slightly and simmer until the chicken is cooked. Remove the saucepan from the stove and place in a cool spot. After 1 hour remove the chicken from the stock and refrigerate. When cold, remove the fillets from the carcass and cut into 1cm-thick slices.

SWEET CORN CUSTARD

3 cobs corn
125ml cream
1 egg
1 yolk
salt
small pinch of cayenne pepper

Preheat the oven to 140°C.

Blanch the corn in a large saucepan of boiling water for 5 minutes. Remove from the saucepan, cut the kernels off the cobs and purée (it is important to purée the corn while still warm).

Measure out 250ml of corn purée and whisk with the cream and eggs. Season with salt and cayenne pepper. Strain the corn custard through a fine sieve and place in a shallow dish. Place in a hot-water bath and cover with tinfoil.

Place in the oven and bake until just set (a few minutes only).

To finish and serve

12 scallops
oil for frying
Watercress and Ginger Sauce (see 'Recipes Continued' on page 191)
pickle for mushrooms (see 'Recipes Continued' on page 191)
sea salt and ground white pepper
2 spring onions, finely chopped

Pan-sear the scallops and arrange 3 on each of 4 large entrée plates, alternating with 3 slices of the cold chicken, 3 small teaspoons of the sauce and 3 quenelles of corn custard. Place 4 pickled mushrooms on each plate. Dust with a pinch of sea salt, a generous amount of ground white pepper and a sprinkling of spring onion rings.

Serves 4

Recipe from Andrew McConnell
THREE, ONE, TWO
MELBOURNE

Recommended wine:
Allies Saone Mornington Peninsula Viognier/Chardonnay 2005

LEFT: *Apertio 53* is an oil on canvas still life study in chiaroscuro by Nona Burden.

Honey Cardamom Glazed Duck Breast

with duck leg dolmades and kumquat jus

HONEY CARDAMOM GLAZE

250ml water
4 cardamom pods, crushed
1 tablespoon honey

Place the ingredients in a saucepan and bring to the boil. Take off the heat and allow to infuse for 2 hours. Strain through a muslin cloth and set aside.

FIG PURÉE

375ml port
250g dried figs

Place the port and figs in a saucepan and simmer until very soft (about 20 minutes). Purée in a food processor and set aside.

KUMQUAT JUS

500g kumquats
500g sugar
250ml water
1 litre duck stock
200ml port

Put the kumquats, sugar and water in a saucepan and bring to the boil. Reduce to a simmer and cook until the kumquats are very soft (almost a marmalade consistency). In a separate saucepan reduce the duck stock to about 300ml. Add the port and kumquats, then set aside.

DOLMADES

4 x size 19 confit duck legs (available from good food stores)
2 tablespoons harissa
2 tablespoons crushed hazelnuts
1 tablespoon ground cinnamon
1 tablespoon chopped parsley
1 tablespoon chopped coriander
12 vine leaves

Shred the duck meat and mix well in a bowl with the harissa, hazelnuts, cinnamon, parsley and coriander. Spoon some of the mixture into the centre of each vine leaf and fold the edges over into the centre, making small parcels (you may need to trim the leaves if there is excess). Roll and press together tightly and set aside.

To finish and serve

4 duck breasts (size 19)
1 handful watercress to garnish

Pan-fry the duck breasts skin-side down until crisp. Turn over and cook for 2 minutes more. Remove from the heat and pour in the glaze, turn the breasts to coat completely, then place skin-side up on a baking rack. Gently pour the remaining glaze over the breasts and allow to rest for 10 minutes.

Microwave the dolmades on High for 3 minutes. Reheat the jus.

Meanwhile, on each plate place 3 spoonfuls of room temperature fig purée and top with 3 dolmades. Slice the duck breasts diagonally and place alongside. Pour some of the jus over and garnish with watercress.

Serves 4

Recipe from Neil Cunningham
SOUK RESTAURANT
MELBOURNE

Recommended wine:
Hurley Vineyard Garamond
Mornington Peninsula Pinot Noir 2004

ABOVE: Port Campbell National Park contains a diverse range of coastal environments including woodlands, dunes, wetlands, coastal cliffs, limestone stacks and arches.

PRICEWATERHOUSECOOPERS

Pan-fried John Dory

with Kipfler potato, green olive and egg salad

SALAD

1 tablespoon currants, soaked overnight in 2 tablespoons orange juice
5 steamed Kipfler potatoes, peeled and diced
1 ½ soft-boiled eggs, diced
6 large green olives, sliced
1 tablespoon pine nuts, toasted
1 tablespoon sesame seeds, toasted
1 teaspoon smoked paprika
½ teaspoon sweet paprika
¼ teaspoon sumac (available from most gourmet delicatessens)
1 teaspoon chopped coriander
1 teaspoon chopped parsley

Mix together all the salad ingredients.

PAN-FRIED JOHN DORY

4 John Dory fillets
4 teaspoons olive tapenade
4 basil leaves, deep-fried

Pan-fry the fillets until caramelised on one side. Turn over and continue to cook for 2 minutes. Do not overcook as the fillets need to be moist in the centre.

To serve

Distribute the salad evenly among 4 plates and place the fish on top. Garnish each with a teaspoon of olive tapenade and a deep-fried basil leaf.

Serves 4

Recipe from Neil Cunningham
SOUK RESTAURANT
MELBOURNE

Recommended wine:
Coombe Farm Yarra Valley
Chardonnay 2004

LEFT: The forecourt of the Melbourne Art Gallery is popular as a gathering place.

Scialatelli Veloci

al pomodoro e basilica

scialatelli pasta (or fresh macaroni)
500g plain flour
500g durum wheat flour
2 eggs
2 tablespoons olive oil
pinch of sea salt
water

Sift and blend the flours, make a well in the centre and add the eggs, oil and sea salt. Mix together to form a dough, adding a little water as needed. Knead for 10 minutes until dough is soft and elastic, but not sticky.

Roll out into logs and cut 2mm-thick pieces on a 45° angle. Form tubes by twisting the pieces around a skewer and cutting into about 10cm lengths. Boil in plenty of salted water until al dente.

TOMATO AND BASIL SAUCE
1/2 cup extra virgin olive oil
2 cloves garlic, peeled and finely chopped
2 punnets juicy cherry tomatoes
sea salt and cracked black pepper
8 fresh basil leaves, sliced if large
1 tablespoon freshly chopped parsley
1 tablespoon freshly chopped oregano

While the scialatelli is cooking, heat the oil in a pan on a high heat and add the garlic. When it starts to colour, add the tomatoes and crush with a fork. Season to taste. Add the basil, parsley and oregano and allow to simmer for a couple of minutes.

Drain the scialatelli well, then toss in the pan with the sauce. Serve immediately.

Serves 8

Recipe from Guy Grossi
GROSSI FLORENTINO
RESTAURANT
MELBOURNE

Recommended wine:
Pizzini King Valley Sangiovese 2003

OPTUS
OPTUS
VICTORIA UNIVERSITY
VICTORIA UNIVERSITY
QBE INSURANCE
DUXTON
HOTEL

PREVIOUS PAGE: A rowing crew trains on the Yarra River, passing the Flinders Street Station.

LEFT: A fanciful, architectural chair created by George Huon.

Pan-fried Gnocchi

with Italian sausage, marinated eggplant and light tomato sugo

GNOCCHI DI PATATE

1kg waxy potatoes
salt to taste
1 ³/₄ cups plain flour

Scrub the potatoes and place them, unpeeled, on a vegetable rack, over a large saucepan of boiling water. Steam until tender. It is important that the potatoes are not overcooked. While they are still hot, peel them and pass them through a vegetable mill into a large bowl. (Don't be tempted to try a food processor for this, it will turn them to glue.)

Add a healthy pinch of salt and the flour to the potatoes. Combine with a wooden spoon, and then knead the dough gently for about 5 minutes on a lightly floured board or wooden work surface. Be careful not to overwork the dough. It should be soft and supple.

Divide the dough into 8 equal pieces. Roll each piece into a rope about 2cm in diameter and 20cm long. Cut each rope into 2cm lengths. If you wish, roll each gnocco over the large holes of a cheese grater or along the tines of a fork to make a pattern in the soft dough.

Bring a large saucepan of lightly salted water to a rolling boil and drop in the gnocchi (doing this in 2 batches may be easier). Boil the gnocchi until they rise to the top, then remove them with a slotted spoon. Transfer the gnocchi to a heated platter or bowl and set aside.

TOMATO SUGO

500g tomatoes
¹/₄ cup olive oil
salt and pepper to taste
1 onion, peeled and finely diced
2 cloves garlic, peeled and crushed
100ml red wine or water

Cut the tomatoes in half, brush with oil and sprinkle with salt and pepper, then roast in the oven at a low temperature (140°C) for 45 minutes. Sauté the onion and garlic in the remaining oil, then add the roasted tomatoes and red wine and simmer for a further 15 minutes over a low heat.

Break up the tomatoes with a wooden spoon and cook until they have melted into a thick, smooth sauce. Take care not to dry out the sauce. It should have a thick, soft consistency. If you prefer a completely smooth sauce, pass it through a food mill or purée roughly in a blender. Set aside.

MARINATED EGGPLANT

2 large eggplants, cut into 3mm-thick horizontal slices
salt and pepper to taste
³/₄ cup extra virgin oil
1 handful chopped parsley
3 cloves garlic, peeled and roughly crushed

Preheat the oven to 200°C. Place the eggplant slices in a colander. If desired, sprinkle with salt and leave for about 30 minutes to allow any bitter juices to drain away. Rinse and pat dry. Place eggplant slices in a tray and bake for 10 minutes on each side, ensuring they are cooked through.

Transfer the eggplant to a plate. Sprinkle with the olive oil, garlic and parsley, and season with salt and pepper to taste. Set aside.

To finish and serve

olive oil for frying
400g Salsiccia Italian sausage cut into 1cm-thick slices
salt and pepper to taste
chopped parsley to garnish

Heat a large, heavy-based frying pan, and brush with a little olive oil. Pan fry the gnocchi in 2 batches over a medium heat for 4–5 minutes, or until golden brown and tender. Cover and keep warm.

Heat the tomato sugo in a saucepan. Add the roughly chopped marinated eggplant and sliced sausage.

Toss gently to combine and heat for 1–2 minutes or until warmed through. Top the gnocchi with the tomato sugo mixture, season with black pepper and garnish with parsley. Serve immediately.

Serves 4

Recipe from Rosemaree Arceri
ANTICA GELATERIA DEL CORSO
MELBOURNE

Recommended wine
Red Hill Estate Mornington Peninsula
Cabernet Sauvignon 2004

Planned to succeed

Australian Capital Territory

CANBERRA, AUSTRALIA'S CAPITAL, has a secret. This meticulously planned city has some of the best cafés and restaurants in the land.

It makes sense. The politicians and bureaucrats who make the place tick travel widely and are used to the best. Little wonder they expect no less in the place where they spend their working days.

Naturally enough in a city where decisions are made that affect the nation, many of the attractions have the word 'National' as part of their name.

Museums, galleries and historic sites attract crowds from around Australia, and from further afield, keen to find out more about the beginnings of this richly diverse country.

The history might come as a surprise. We tend to think that nothing much happened in the region before politicians decided to build a new capital city there in the early 1900s. In fact, the indigenous culture was strong, and there was also an active farming community.

Canberra was designed as a city in a park, so naturally public art is part of the local vernacular.

And speaking of parks, the Australian Institute of Sport offers visitors the opportunity to be guided around the complex by one of the athletes who train there.

Science and technology also play an important part in the region's development, and visitors are encouraged to increase their knowledge. The National Science and Technology Centre offers the chance to experience a man-made earthquake or get close to a lightning bolt among its many attractions.

Wine is made by a number of producers, and despite the fact that most companies are tiny, some labels are gaining a good reputation outside the region. Many wineries offer cellar door tastings, and some have an attached café or restaurant. Few are more than 30 minutes' drive from the city centre.

LEFT: Canberra is a city in a park, a landscaped capital carefully designed to transform with the turn of each distinct season.

Rare Roasted Saddle of Delegate River Venison

with pumpkin and walnut ravioli and blueberry sauce

4 x 160g pieces Delegate River venison saddle
olive oil
cinnamon stick
aniseed
freshly ground black pepper
juniper berries
sage
bay leaves

Combine all the ingredients and marinate overnight.

PUMPKIN AND WALNUT RAVIOLI
85g pumpkin, skin on
50g chopped walnuts
20g Parmigiano Reggiano, grated
salt and freshly ground black pepper
8 pasta rounds (see 'Recipes Continued' on page 191)
1 egg, beaten
8 tablespoons clarified butter
6 fresh chopped sage leaves

Preheat the oven to 150°C. Wrap the pumpkin in tinfoil and bake for 30 minutes. Cut the flesh away from the skin and purée in a blender. Pass through a fine strainer into a square of muslin. Tie up the ends and suspend to drain for 1 hour.

Mix together the pumpkin purée, walnuts and Parmigiano Reggiano and season with salt and pepper.

Place the rounds of dough on a well-floured bench and put 2 tablespoons in the centre of each 8cm round. Brush the edges with egg, then place the 10cm rounds on top. Using a 5cm cutter, press the outside down and seal.

Set aside on a tray dusted with semolina and cover with a cloth until needed.

BLUEBERRY SAUCE
150ml chicken jus
140g fresh blueberries
20g butter cubes

Heat the jus and reduce by two-thirds. Add the blueberries and whisk in the butter. Process in a blender.

SLOW-ROASTED SAVOY CABBAGE
40ml goose fat
280g finely sliced Savoy cabbage, blanched and refreshed
20g black truffle, finely sliced
salt and freshly ground black pepper

Place the goose fat into a hot pan and melt. Add the cabbage and truffle and season. Sauté for 3–4 minutes until tender.

To finish and serve
oil and butter for frying

Preheat the oven to 200°C. Remove the venison from the marinade and season each piece on both sides. Seal in a hot pan in a little oil until golden on both sides. Add a little butter, let it foam then baste the venison.

Roast the meat in the oven for 3 minutes. Take out and rest until needed. Slice thinly.

Blanch the ravioli in boiling, salted water, then reduce heat and cook for about 2 more minutes. Drain and toss in clarified butter, sage and salt and pepper.

Arrange a bed of cabbage on each plate and place the sliced venison on this with ravioli on top. Pour the blueberry sauce around.

Serves 4

Recipe from Daren Tetley
THE BOAT HOUSE BY THE LAKE
CANBERRA

Recommended wine:
Yarra Burn Yarra Valley Shiraz 2003

ABOVE: The interior of Parliament House in Canberra features various native timbers and hosts numerous pieces of Australian art and craft.

White Chocolate and Baileys Soufflé

with banana ice cream

250ml milk
50ml Baileys
75g white chocolate
300g caster sugar plus extra for dusting
50g cornflour
2 egg yolks
200g (about 7) egg whites
butter for greasing

Preheat the oven to 190°C. Bring the milk and Baileys to the boil.

Put the white chocolate in a saucepan over a bain-marie to melt, whisking continuously.

Place one-third of the sugar, plus the cornflour and egg yolks in a saucepan and slowly mix in the milk and Baileys mixture to make a crème pâtisserie. Simmer over a low heat until thick and smooth.

Whisk the egg whites to stiff peaks and slowly add the remaining sugar.

Butter 4 ramekins and dust with sugar.

Gently fold together one part crème pâtisserie to two parts egg white and pour into each ramekin. Run a knife around the edges. Place in the oven for 10–12 minutes.

BANANA ICE CREAM

40g ripe bananas, puréed
100ml milk
100ml cream
5ml banana liqueur
50g sugar
2 egg yolks
dried banana chips to serve

Combine the banana, milk, cream and banana liqueur, and infuse over a low heat for 30 minutes. Remove from heat and strain.

Cream the sugar and egg yolks, then whisk into the strained mixture. Cook over a low heat until it coats the back of a spoon. Strain and chill over an ice bath. Place in an ice cream machine and churn until frozen. Serve with dried banana chips.

Serves 4

Recipe from Daren Tetley
THE BOAT HOUSE BY THE LAKE
CANBERRA

Recommended wine:
Lake George Tokay 1999

Fattoush

(Lebanese bread salad)

100g piece day-old Turkish bread
90ml mild blend olive oil
salt and freshly ground black pepper
1 clove garlic, peeled (optional)
30ml red wine vinegar
½ small red onion, peeled and finely sliced
3 super-ripe, super-sweet tomatoes, cored and cut into 8 pieces
1 avocado, peeled, stoned and diced into 2cm cubes
1 Continental cucumber, peeled and diced into 2cm cubes
1 spring onion, finely chopped
I cup flat-leaf parsley leaves
1 cup coriander leaves
8 mint leaves, torn into smallish pieces
1 teaspoon sumac

Preheat the oven to 160°C. Break the bread into 2–3cm chunks, toss in some of the olive oil, season with salt and pepper and toast in the oven until dry, golden and crunchy (20–30 minutes, depending on the thickness). Rub each piece with a cut garlic clove (optional).

Make a simple vinaigrette by combining the red wine vinegar and a mild olive oil in equal quantities. Season well with salt and pepper.

Soak the red onion in cold water for a few minutes to help release some of the acid.

To finish and serve
In a large stainless steel bowl, coat the toasted bread with red wine vinaigrette and leave to soak for about 2 minutes. Squeeze the red onion to release the water and add to the bowl along with all the prepared vegetables. Season well with salt and pepper and toss gently. Add the herbs and sumac, toss again and serve.

Serves 1

Recipe from Cath Claringbold
MECCA BAH
CANBERRA

Recommended wine:
James Estate Hunter Valley Verdelho 2005

BELOW: Colin Lanceley created *Shoal* with oil and carved wood on canvas.

Moroccan Spiced Calamari

with Turkish bean salad

8 medium calamari tubes, cleaned
1 small clove garlic, peeled
1 small hot red chilli
1 sprig fresh oregano
1 teaspoon ground cumin
2 teaspoons sweet paprika
pinch of saffron
½ teaspoon caster sugar
lemon juice
olive oil
salt to taste
1 x 400g can cannellini beans
250g green beans, blanched
200g semi-dried or oven-roasted tomatoes
½ small red onion, peeled and very thinly sliced
1 tablespoon chopped mint
1 tablespoon chopped parsley
200ml lemon vinaigrette (70ml lemon juice whisked with 130ml olive oil)
finely ground salt and black pepper
lemon wedges to serve

Using a sharp knife, cut the calamari tubes down one side from the inside out. Open like a book and score the flesh diagonally to make a criss-cross pattern, being careful not to cut all the way through (the knife tip should sink in only a quarter of the depth of the flesh and the cuts should be 5mm apart). Cut the calamari into 8cm x 8cm squares.

Pound the garlic, chilli and oregano in a mortar and pestle, then add the cumin, paprika, saffron, caster sugar, a good splash of lemon juice and olive oil to make a paste the consistency of wet sand. Season.

Place the scored calamari in a bowl and coat completely with the marinade, rubbing it in well with your fingers.

Combine the remaining ingredients in a stainless steel bowl and season well.

Place the calamari pieces scored-side down in a hot pan with a dash of olive oil. Do not overcrowd the pan so cook in batches or in 2 pans. As the calamari cooks it will begin to curl. Once curled, roll it around the pan to get an even colour all over. Do not overcook, or it will become chewy and tough. If the pan is hot to begin with, the total cooking time will be under 2 minutes.

To serve
Divide the salad between 4 plates and place the calamari pieces on top. Serve with a wedge of lemon.

Serves 4

Recipe from Cath Claringbold
MECCA BAH
CANBERRA

Recommended wine:
Clonakilla Canberra District Riesling 2005

RIGHT: *Magnolia Plate* crafted by Mitsuo Shoji.

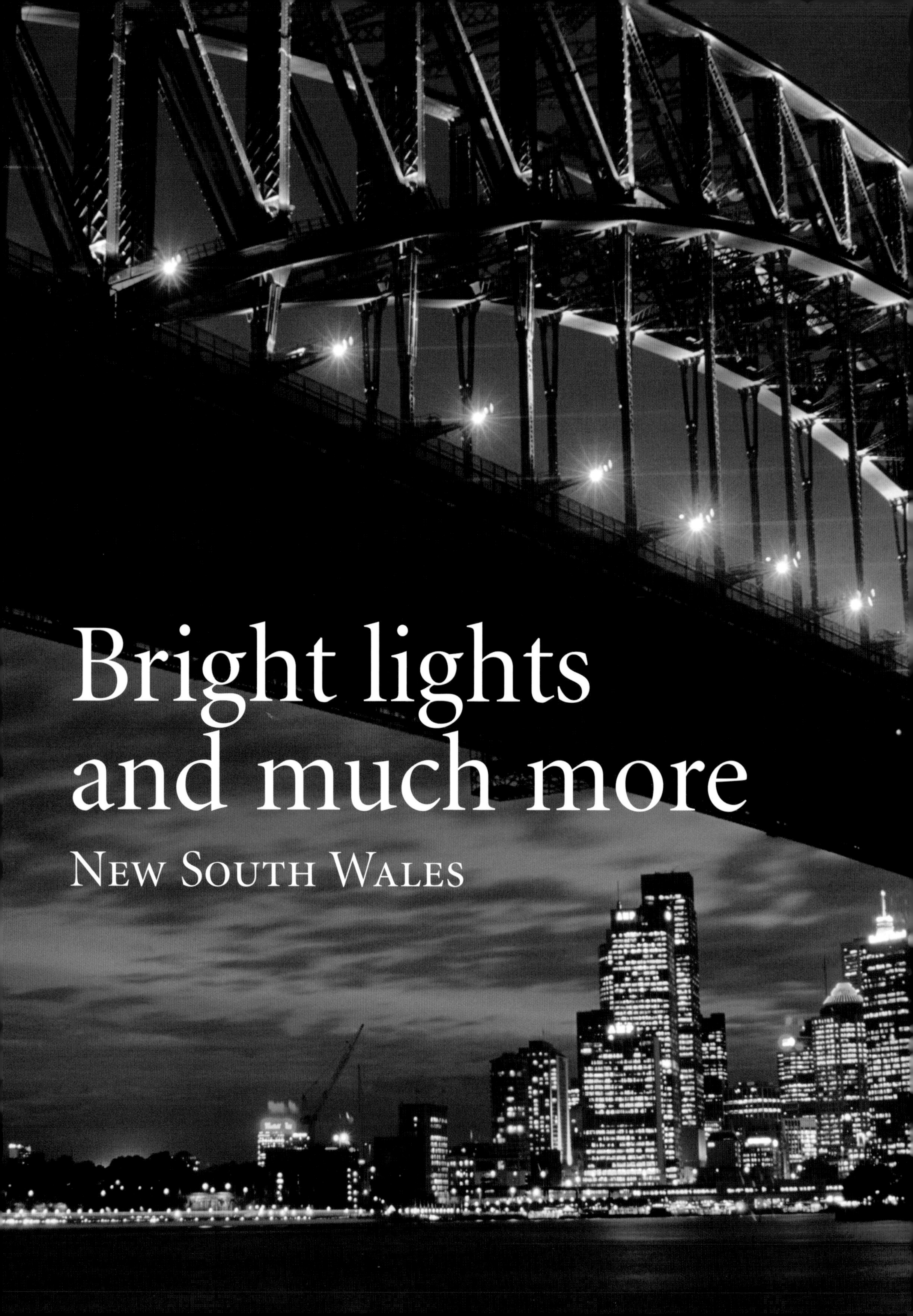
Bright lights
and much more
New South Wales

THINK NEW SOUTH WALES, think Sydney. This somewhat blinkered attitude is an inevitable result of the state's having the country's biggest centre of population – more than Western Australia, South Australia and Tasmania put together – but New South Wales has a great deal more to commend it than the bright lights of Sydney.

Not that there is anything wrong with a fascination with one of the world's great cities. Sydney boasts two internationally famous landmarks, the Harbour Bridge and the Opera House, as well as many examples of public art.

It is also one of the world's great restaurant cities. Literally thousands of cafés and restaurants, many of them lauded overseas as well as throughout the land, offer food from the cuisines of the world.

Sydney was also the birthplace of the Australian wine industry. The country's first vines were planted at Farm Cove, and the first export wine left the city's shores, bound for England, in 1823.

Nowadays, wine lovers head for the Hunter Valley, where wines made from the Semillon grape are revered for their ability to age with grace and poise. Hunter reds also enjoy a great reputation, and overseas visitors are intrigued by the term 'sweaty saddle', used to describe one of their unique attributes. Wine is also produced in Mudgee, not far from the Hunter, and the Murrumbidgee Irrigation Area, far to the west.

Away from the Hunter's well-established wine cellars and back into the sun-soaked outdoors, beaches string out along the coast north of the city, while to the south the Blue Mountains attract trampers and lovers of wildlife.

New South Wales has an enthusiastic and active art community. At the Art Gallery of New South Wales, collections of classical and contemporary art from Australian, European and Asian artists change regularly and invariably attract big crowds.

LEFT: Sydney Harbour Bridge celebrates its 75th anniversary in 2007. The widest long-span bridge in the world, it also has the world's largest steel arch.

ABOVE *Rushcutters Bay*, an oil on canvas work by Nicole Southworth.

Poached King George Whiting

with prawn and parsnip brandade

BRANDADE

2 medium-sized potatoes (Désirée or Sebago variety)
2 parsnips, peeled and cored
4 cloves garlic, peeled
100ml milk
150ml olive oil
200g dry salt cod, soaked overnight in cold water
salt and white milled pepper

Cut the potatoes and parsnips into quarters, and place with the garlic in a saucepan over the heat and cover with cold salted water. When fully cooked and soft, drain and peel, wearing kitchen gloves to handle them. Mash the cooked vegetables with the milk first and then add the olive oil to thin down. Season and put aside.

Poach the salt cod pieces for 10 minutes and allow them to cool. Drain and remove the skin, bones and fatty parts. Flake into small pieces and add to the mashed potato. Reheat and adjust the consistency with oil and a touch of the cod poaching liquid. Check the seasoning.

WHITE WINE SAUCE

6 shallots, peeled and sliced
2 cloves garlic, peeled and thinly sliced
60ml olive oil
100ml white wine
200ml fish stock
1 handful parsley, sorrel and thyme stalks
12 black peppercorns, cracked
400ml cream
salt and white milled pepper

Sweat the shallots and the garlic in the olive oil without colouring. Add the white wine and reduce to one-third. Add the fish stock and reduce by one-third. Add the herbs and the peppercorns, then add the cream and reduce it by half until you achieve a creamy sauce consistency. Strain and season.

8 fillets King George whiting, pin bones removed
knob of butter
salt and pepper
250ml fish stock
4 large prawns, peeled
1 handful chervil, frisée lettuce or curly endive and other little leaves
2 tablespoons vinaigrette

Preheat the oven to 150°C. Butter a flat roasting tray. Lay the whiting fillets skin down in the tray, and season to taste. Drizzle with a little fish stock without completely covering the fillets. Wrap the tray in tinfoil. Bake the fish for 5 minutes.

Sear the prawns in a little butter or oil, season and set aside. Toss the chervil and lettuce in the vinaigrette and reserve.

To serve

2 tablespoons olive oil
4 baby fennel, blanched
2 tomatoes, blanched, deseeded, peeled and quartered
extra olive oil

Put a scoop of Brandade in a deep bowl, place a drained fish fillet on this and top with some lettuce. Serve with the white wine sauce and a good drizzle of olive oil. Garnish with the fennel and tomato, lightly warmed up in a touch of olive oil.

Serves 4

Recipe from Serge Dansereau
BATHERS PAVILION
SYDNEY

Recommended wine:

Thomas Braemore Hunter Valley Semillon 2005

Kangaroo Island Freshwater Marron Bouillabaisse

BOUILLABAISSE STOCK

500g flathead
500g blue swimmer crabs
500g leatherjacket
500g rock cod
1 small bulb fennel, chopped
1 small onion, peeled and chopped
1 small leek, chopped
4 tomatoes, chopped
1 teaspoon fennel seeds
1 teaspoon coriander seeds
pinch of saffron
pinch of sea salt
1 teaspoon freshly ground black pepper
2 litres fish stock
1 bay leaf
2 sprigs thyme
6 cloves garlic, crushed with skin on
2 tablespoons tomato paste
200ml Pernod

Cut the fish into large pieces and place in a large stockpot with the rest of the ingredients. Bring to the boil and cook at a fast simmer for 2 hours. Pass through a mouli or press as much as you can through a chinois or sieve into another saucepan. Reserve.

ROUILLE

1 small potato, peeled and chopped
½ red capsicum
½ bird's eye chilli
pinch of saffron
200ml bouillabaisse stock
2 egg yolks
1 clove garlic, peeled and finely chopped
150ml extra virgin olive oil
1 tablespoon Dijon mustard

Place the potato, capsicum, chilli, saffron and stock in a saucepan and simmer over a low heat until the potato is cooked. Press through a sieve and allow to cool. Whisk in the egg yolks, mustard and garlic, then gradually whisk in the olive oil.

BOUILLABAISSE

4 whole small flatheads, gutted and scaled
2 whole green blue swimmer crabs
4 whole red mullets, gutted and scaled
400g clams
4 x 100g blue eye fillets
4 tomatoes, peeled, deseeded and diced
pinch of salt
2 litres bouillabaisse stock
500g yabbies

Put all the ingredients except the yabbies in a large saucepan. Bring to a fierce boil for 5 minutes. Add the yabbies and serve immediately with rouille on the side.

NOTE: The essential accompaniment for bouillabaisse, rouille, which means 'rust' in French owing to its lovely orange colour, should be garlicky with a bit of heat from the chilli. It can also be served spread on toast with a poached egg or as a dip with crisp sourdough or with steamed John Dory fillet.

Serves 4

Recipe from Perry Hill
THE BOATHOUSE
ON BLACKWATTLE BAY
SYDNEY

Recommended wine:
Estio Rosado Yecla 2005 (Spain)

LEFT: Bondi is one of Australia's most famous and popular surf beaches and is a great place for scuba diving.

TOP: *Maroubra Beach*, acrylic on canvas by Andrew Taylor.

BOTTOM: Kerry Lester painted *The Swimmer* in acrylic on board.

Pear Soufflé

with chocolate sorbet and chantilly cream

CHANTILLY CREAM
100ml cream
40g icing sugar
1 vanilla bean

Whisk the cream with the icing sugar and the seeds scraped from the vanilla pod.

PEAR SOUFFLÉ
250g pears, peeled and cored
195g sugar plus extra for moulds
250ml water
6 eggs, separated
butter to grease moulds
pinch of salt
120g sugar

Put the pears in a saucepan with 75g of sugar and the water. Bring to the boil and boil for 5 minutes. Blend and pass through a fine sieve.

Preheat the oven to 160°C. Butter 4 soufflé moulds and coat with sugar. In a bowl place 120ml of the pear mixture (there will be some left over), 60g of sugar and the egg yolks, and whisk gently.

Beat the egg whites in a copper or glass bowl with a pinch of salt, then add the remaining 60g of sugar. Whisk until soft peaks form. Pour half into the pear mixture and mix a little. Add the rest of the egg whites and mix with a spatula. Pour into the moulds and level with a spatula. Bake for 8 minutes.

Serve with chantilly cream and chocolate sorbet (See 'Recipes Continued', page 191) on the side.

Serves 4

Recipe from Perry Hill
THE BOATHOUSE
ON BLACKWATTLE BAY
SYDNEY

Recommended wine:
Camyr Allyn Wines
Hunter Valley Verdelho 2005

ABOVE: *Ceramic study and lemons* is a work by Vincent Ko in acrylic on canvas.

Macquarie Harbour Ocean Trout Roe

with potato blinis and crème fraîche

400g potatoes, peeled and cut in chunks
2 eggs
1 teaspoon crème fraîche plus extra for serving
2 egg whites
1 tablespoon plain flour
2 tablespoons clarified butter (see 'Recipes Continued' on page 191) or ghee
200g Macquarie Harbour salmon roe
2 lemons, cut into wedges
wasabi to serve

Cook the potatoes in a steamer for 45 minutes. Crack the eggs into a bowl and add the crème fraîche. When the potatoes are cooked, pass through a mouli (or press through a sieve until smooth), then weigh out 250g.

Add the flour, then mix in the egg mixture. Beat the egg whites until stiff and combine gently with the potato mixture. Refrigerate for 1 hour.

Heat a non-stick frying pan, add some clarified butter then pour in spoonfuls of the blini batter and cook on both sides until golden brown.

Serve the blini immediately spread with crème fraîche and topped with the salmon roe, a wedge of lemon on the side and some wasabi.

Serves 4

Recipe from Perry Hill
THE BOATHOUSE ON BLACKWATTLE BAY
SYDNEY

Recommended wine:
Champagne Henriot (France)

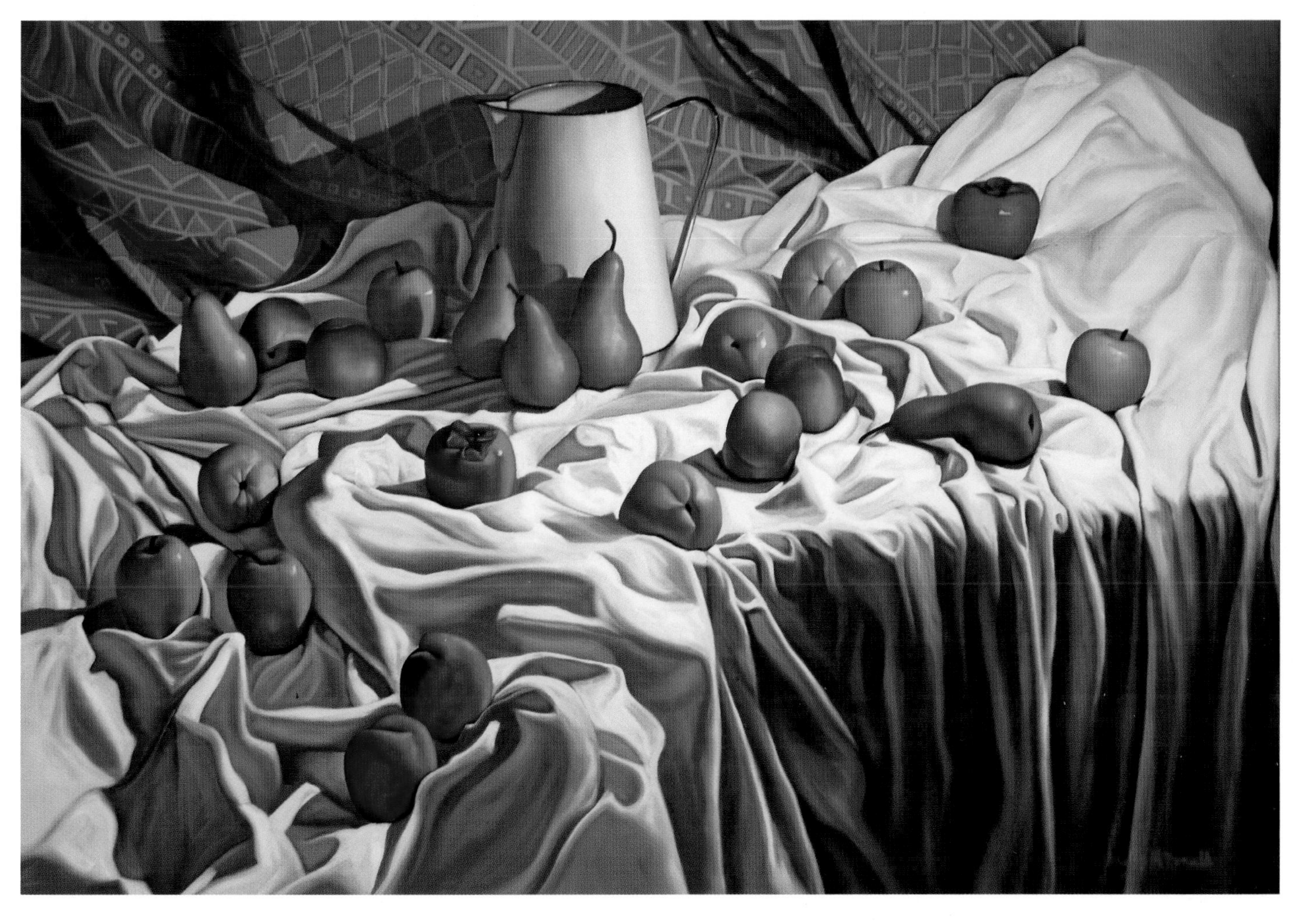

ABOVE: *Still Life with Fruit,* an oil on canvas work by Angus McDonald.

Mosaic of Snowy Mountain Rabbit

with cabbage, foie gras and shiitake mushrooms

1 whole rabbit
1/3 cup rock salt
1 bunch thyme
1 tablespoon black peppercorns
2 litres duck fat

Combine all the ingredients except the duck fat. Mix well and refrigerate overnight.

Preheat the oven to 120°C. Wash the rabbit in cold water and place in a baking dish with the duck fat. Cook for 4 hours or until the meat falls off the bone.

TERRINE
1kg shiitake mushrooms, sliced
1kg Chinese cabbage, sliced
oil or butter
salt and freshly ground black pepper
1 litre brown chicken stock
1 1/2 tablespoons gelatine
200g foie gras
2kg Kipfler potatoes, cooked and peeled
1/3 cup chopped chives
truffle oil to serve

Sauté the mushrooms and cabbage in a little oil or butter until soft. Season well with salt and pepper. Place in a colander to drain off any excess liquid.

Heat 100ml of the stock and dissolve the gelatine in this. Add the rest of the stock. Cool to room temperature.

Cut the rabbit meat, foie gras and potatoes into 2.5cm-wide x 5cm-long batons.

Line a terrine mould or loaf tin with plastic cling film. Drizzle a little stock and sprinkle some chives into the mould, then build layers of mushroom and cabbage mixture, and foie gras, rabbit and potato batons. Repeat in that order until the mould is full (3 layers of each). Refrigerate for 24 hours.

To turn out the terrine, place the mould in a hot-water bath for 20 seconds (without water getting onto the terrine), then turn out onto a board. Slice with a serrated knife and brush with truffle oil to serve.

Serves 12

Recipe from Grant Kell
LA GRANDE BOUFFE
SYDNEY

Recommended wine:
Coriole Vineyards McLaren Vale
Nebbiolo Rosé 2006

ABOVE: The Blue Mountains is the only World Heritage region on the edge of a major city (Sydney) and offers a wealth of outdoor activities including bush walking, cycling and rock climbing.

Roast Mandagery Creek Venison Loin

with a trio of purées and raspberry and chocolate sauce

1 whole venison loin
red wine

Cut the venison into eight 120–140g portions. Marinate in red wine for 24 hours.

TRIO OF PURÉES

1 butternut pumpkin, deseeded, peeled and cut into chunks
1 celeriac, peeled and cut into chunks
salt to taste
100ml milk
3 beetroot, peeled

Cook the pumpkin and celeriac separately until tender in enough boiling water to cover. Drain, add salt and 50ml milk to each, and cool. Purée the vegetables separately. Cook the beetroot until tender in boiling water to cover, season and purée.

RASPBERRY AND CHOCOLATE SAUCE

2kg venison bones
3 carrots, coarsely chopped
3 onions, peeled and coarsely chopped
1 head celery, coarsely chopped
2 litres wine
veal stock
1 litre raspberry vinegar
60g peppercorns, cracked
5g dark chocolate (70% cocoa), grated

Roast the venison bones with the carrots, onions and celery. Add the wine, place on moderate heat and simmer until reduced by two-thirds. Add enough veal stock to cover the bones, then simmer for 6 hours. Pass the jus through a fine sauce.

Heat the vinegar and peppercorns in a clean saucepan and simmer until reduced by two-thirds, then add to the jus. Reduce again by half then add the dark chocolate.

To finish and serve

oil
Brussels sprouts or glazed apple to garnish

Preheat the oven to 180°C. Sear the venison portions in a little oil in a very hot pan for 3 minutes each side, then place in the oven for 2 minutes. Remove from the oven and let the meat rest for 5 minutes. Repeat until all the pieces are cooked.

Place a mound of each purée on each serving plate. Slice the venison portions into 3, arrange on the purées and drizzle with the sauce. Garnish with Brussels sprouts or glazed apple.

Serves 8

Recipe from Grant Kell
LA GRANDE BOUFFE
SYDNEY

Recommended wine:

Bannockburn Geelong Shiraz 2003

Antipasto Crudo

For this dish you will need the freshest seasonal seafood from a good fishmonger or fish market.

4 scallops in the half shell
100g sashimi-grade yellowfin tuna
100g sashimi-grade ocean trout
100g sashimi-grade swordfish
100g sashimi-grade Hirimasa kingfish

Neatly slice all the fish and the scallops into 5mm-thick slices except the kingfish, which should be sliced carpaccio style i.e. as thinly as possible.

SWORDFISH GARNISH
50g mayonnaise
squeeze of lemon juice
1 handful parsley, chopped
10 capers, coarsely chopped
1 tomato, cut into 4, then diced into 5mm cubes

SCALLOP GARNISH
1 red chilli, finely chopped
1 clove garlic, peeled and finely chopped
½ bunch chives, finely chopped
squeeze of lemon juice

KINGFISH GARNISH
½ bulb fennel, shaved
1 orange, peeled and cut into segments
juice of 1 lemon
20g pine nuts, toasted

TUNA GARNISH
½ cucumber, peeled and cut into ribbons with a vegetable peeler

OCEAN TROUT GARNISH
1 handful rocket salad, washed
lemon oil

To finish and serve
extra virgin olive oil
salt and freshly ground black pepper

Make up the swordfish garnish first. Place the mayo, lemon juice, chopped parsley and capers into a bowl. Mix well. Add the diced tomato. Place 4 slices of swordfish on the work surface, spoon a little of the mixture onto each, then roll up and refrigerate.

In 5 small bowls, place a little olive oil and salt and pepper. Put each garnish mixture including the swordfish into a bowl and toss.

Arrange on 4 serving plates, except for the scallop garnish; add the sliced scallop meat to the bowl, toss and divide among the washed scallop shells then place one on each plate. Toss the different fish in their respective bowls and arrange on their garnishes. Drizzle each bowl with extra virgin olive oil and serve.

Serves 4

Recipe from Daniel Hughes
MANTA RESTAURANT
SYDNEY

Recommended wine:
Logan Wines Orange Sauvignon Blanc 2005

BELOW: Pelicans are found throughout Australia and are opportunistic feeders. They eat a variety of aquatic animals including fish, crustaceans, tadpoles and turtles, as well as readily accepting handouts from humans.

chardonnay, 2004

Whole Baked Garfish

on caponata

1 medium eggplant, cut into 1cm cubes
salt
100g pine nuts
1 medium onion, peeled and finely chopped
3 sticks celery, finely chopped
1 red capsicum, cored, deseeded and finely chopped
50ml white wine
olive oil for frying
100g pitted green olives, coarsely chopped
zest and juice of 1 lemon
100g currants, soaked in a little balsamic vinegar
1 handful flat-leaf parsley, coarsely chopped
4 garfish, butterflied (ask your fishmonger to do this)
salt and pepper to taste
lemon wedges to serve

Lightly salt the eggplant and leave on kitchen paper for 20 minutes to draw out some of the moisture.

Toast the pine nuts in a dry pan over a low, even heat (this draws out the natural oils, enhancing the flavour).

Heat a little olive oil in a saucepan, add the onion and sweat for 6–8 minutes. Add the celery and cook for a further 2 minutes, then add the capsicum. Cook for 1 minute. Add the white wine, cook for 2 minutes, then remove from the heat. Transfer to a bowl.

Deep-fry the eggplant until golden brown then drain on kitchen paper. Add to the capsicum mix along with the olives, lemon zest and juice, drained currants and parsley. Toss caponata well and set aside.

Preheat the oven to 180°C. Season the fish on both sides. Lightly drizzle a non-stick oven tray with some olive oil. Place the fish skin-side up on the tray and bake for 6–8 minutes until just cooked, taking care not to overcook. Squeeze a little lemon juice over.

ABOVE: *Tommy Ruff for Dinner* is an oil painting on linen by Jasmine Symons.

To serve
Spread some caponata on each plate and place the fish on top. Garnish with a lemon wedge and serve.

Serves 4

Recipe from Daniel Hughes
MANTA RESTAURANT
SYDNEY

Recommended wine:
Manta by Farr Chardonnay 2004

ABOVE: A horse-drawn carriage awaits prospective tourists under the shadow of Sydney Harbour Bridge at The Rocks.

Croque Madame with Chilli Jam

CHILLI JAM

4 red capsicums, deseeded, cored and cut into 3cm squares
3 red onions, peeled and cut into 3cm squares
20 cloves garlic, peeled
5cm knob ginger, thinly sliced
8 red bird's eye chillies, stems removed
400ml vegetable or olive oil
20 large basil leaves
5 medium ripe tomatoes, coarsely chopped
$^{1}/_{2}$ cup sugar
75ml fish sauce

Place the capsicum, onion, garlic, ginger and chillies in a cast-iron frying pan and add the oil. Place over a medium-hot heat and cook for 20–30 minutes, stirring periodically. When the ingredients have become dark golden, add the basil and tomato. Cook for a further 15 minutes over a moderate heat, then add the sugar and fish sauce. Cook over a high heat, stirring, for 3 minutes, then remove from the heat. Strain off any excess oil, then pour the mixture into a food processor and purée. Store in the refrigerator when cool. Will keep for 2–3 months.

CROQUE MADAME

1 bâtarde white loaf (or quality white bread of choice)
softened butter
20 slices Heidi gruyère cheese
16 slices good quality ham
4 fried eggs (with yolks a little runny)
rocket to serve

Slice the bread into 8 toast-thick slices. Spread each slice with butter on one side. Place 4 slices butter-side down on a chopping board. Place 3 slices of cheese, then 2 slices of ham on each slice, followed by a fried egg, then the remaining 2 slices of ham and finally 2 more cheese slices (this will melt and bind the sandwich when pan-frying). Top with the remaining slices of bread, butter-side up.

Melt a little butter in a frying pan and gently pan-fry the croques until golden brown. Turn over and finish in the oven at 180°C for 5–7 minutes.

Serve the croque madame with a rocket garnish and chilli jam.

Serves 4

Recipe from Lorraine Godsmark
YELLOW FOOD STORE
SYDNEY

Recommended drink: great with coffee

Strawberry Mascarpone Cake

COCONUT MERINGUE
60g almond meal
140g desiccated coconut
120g shredded coconut
380g egg whites (about large 14 eggs)
130g caster sugar
280g pure icing sugar, sifted, plus extra for dusting

Preheat the oven to 150°C. Line a Swiss roll tin with greaseproof paper. Combine the almond meal with both types of coconut.

Beat the egg whites to firm peaks, then gradually beat in the caster sugar. Fold the icing sugar in with your hand, then follow with the almond and coconut mix until well combined. It is important to do this slowly but efficiently to maintain the volume.

Spread into the tin, dust with extra icing sugar and bake for 30 minutes. When cool, cut into thirds horizontally.

MASCARPONE FILLING
1kg mascarpone
100g caster sugar
3 eggs, separated
50g caster sugar

Place the mascarpone, first measure of sugar and egg yolks in a mixer and beat until firm.

In a separate bowl beat the whites with the second measure of sugar to firm peaks. Fold half of this meringue into the mascarpone mix, then fold in the remainder.

To finish and serve
2 punnets strawberries, halved
icing sugar for dusting

Place the first meringue disc on a board and cover with an entrement ring (stainless steel cake ring). Fill with half the mascarpone mixture. Press half the strawberries into this mix.

Place a second meringue disc on top and cover with the remaining mascarpone and strawberries. Top with the last meringue disc and refrigerate overnight.

Before serving, dust with icing sugar and caramelise with a blowtorch.

Serves 12–15

Recipe from Lorraine Godsmark
YELLOW FOOD STORE
SYDNEY

Recommended wine:
Primitivo Quiles Moscatel
Vino de Licor (Spain)

RIGHT: The old and the new on George Street, Sydney.

Steamed Marron Tails

with tomato and fennel relish and a turmeric jus

TOMATO AND FENNEL RELISH

75ml olive oil
1 brown onion, peeled and finely diced
2 cloves garlic, peeled and finely diced
3 fennel bulbs, halved and simmered for 20 minutes, finely diced
8 vine-ripened tomatoes, skinned, deseeded and finely diced
30ml lemon juice
salt and pepper

Heat the oil and sauté the onion and garlic until translucent. Add the fennel and then fold in the tomato. Season with the lemon juice, salt and pepper.

TURMERIC JUS

1 small Spanish onion, peeled and cut into small dice
50ml grape seed oil
1 Granny Smith apple, peeled and cut into small dice
1 tablespoon ground turmeric
100ml water
100g butter, softened
300ml light fish stock
30ml lemon juice
salt and pepper

In a saucepan, sauté the onion with the grape seed oil. Add the apple, turmeric and water, and cook for 10 minutes. Cool, purée, then pass through a fine sieve. Fold in the butter and refrigerate.

To make the jus, lightly heat the fish stock and whisk in the purée. Season with lemon juice, salt and pepper.

BASIL OIL

1 1/2 cups basil leaves
200ml olive oil

Blanch the basil and refresh in cold water. Purée the basil with the oil and then strain through cheesecloth.

To finish and serve

6 marron tails, in the shell
fennel fronds to garnish

Steam the marron tails for 5 minutes. Cut out of the shells.

Spoon some tomato and fennel relish onto each serving plate. Add a small amount of potato purée if you wish. Place a marron tail on top and drizzle with the turmeric jus, then pour on a small amount of basil oil. Garnish with fennel fronds.

Serves 6

Recipe from George Sinclair
YELLOW BISTRO
SYDNEY

Recommended wine:
Brown Brothers
Pinot Grigio 2005

RIGHT: Bronze sculpture by Henry Moore, *Reclining Figure – Angles* 1980. Art Gallery of New South Wales.

LEFT: *Off The Grid* is a textile artwork using silk and various threads, by Maz Beeston.

Pancetta-wrapped Roast Duck

with caramelised apple, celeriac purée and roast eshallots

80g butter
3 Golden Delicious apples, peeled, cored and each cut into 6 wedges
2 tablespoons sugar
50ml balsamic vinegar
freshly ground black pepper
6 skinned duck breasts
50g sliced pancetta

Melt half the butter in a pan. Add the apples and toss with 1 teaspoon of the sugar. Increase the heat, continuing to add more butter and sugar. Toss periodically until golden and glazed. Sprinkle with balsamic vinegar and pepper, then set aside to cool.

Butterfly the duck breasts, taking care not to cut all the way through. Place 3 apple segments on each breast, season with a little black pepper, roll up and wrap in pancetta.

CELERIAC PURÉE

500g celeriac, peeled and cut into large pieces
milk to cover
1 clove garlic, peeled and crushed
25ml lemon juice
50ml extra virgin olive oil
salt and freshly ground pepper

Place the celeriac and garlic in a saucepan and add just enough milk to cover. Simmer for about 20 minutes then strain, reserving the liquid. Cover the celeriac with a cloth to keep warm and steam.

Place the warm celeriac in a food processor, add 50ml of the warm cooking liquid and the lemon juice. Blend and, with the motor running, slowly add the olive oil until incorporated. Adjust the seasoning and keep warm.

To finish and serve

oil for frying
250ml light chicken stock
50ml verjuice
salt and freshly ground black pepper
Roast Eschallots (see 'Recipes Continued' on page 191)
sorrel or basil to garnish

Preheat the oven to 180°C. Sear the duck breasts in a pan with a little oil then roast for 8 minutes, turning while cooking. Allow to rest for 5 minutes.

Place the stock and verjuice in a small saucepan, bring to a simmer then season with salt and pepper.

Place a mound of celeriac purée on each plate with 3 heated eschallots (halved) mixed with some sorrel or basil. Slice the duck and place on the purée, and ladle a little heated sauce over the top.

Serves 6

Recipe from George Sinclair
YELLOW BISTRO
SYDNEY

Recommended wine:
Mount Horrocks Clare Valley
Cabernet Merlot 2001

Recipes Continued

Angel Hair Pasta

(from page 38)

150g plain flour
$^1/_2$ teaspoon salt
2 egg yolks
1 egg
1 teaspoon olive oil
2 teaspoons water

Place the flour and salt in a food processor. Add the eggs and oil and process, slowly adding the water, until the dough has a breadcrumb texture. Tip out on a lightly floured surface and knead until smooth, then wrap in plastic cling film and allow to rest for at least 30 minutes.

Roll the dough through a pasta machine at number 4. Fold and roll through again, then pass through the machine at number 6. Add the angel hair attachment and roll through. Let the pasta hang to dry for at least 10 minutes.

Dipping Sauce

(from page 55)

100ml hoisin sauce
30ml rice wine vinegar
1 tablespoon caster sugar
1 tablespoon ground roasted peanuts

Combine the hoisin, vinegar and sugar, and mix until the sugar is dissolved. Place in 4 small condiment dishes and sprinkle with the ground peanuts.

Tuscan Pesto

(from page 73)

2 cups basil leaves
1 cup thyme leaves
1 cup oregano leaves
1 cup marjoram leaves
2 cups flat-leaf parsley leaves
12 cloves garlic, peeled and minced
1 $^1/_2$ teaspoons salt
1 teaspoon ground white pepper
100g almond meal
almond oil
vegetable oil

Blend together all the ingredients except the oils, then add enough of each oil to make a paste to the desired consistency.

Mayonnaise

(from page 74)

3 egg yolks
1 teaspoon English mustard
$^1/_2$ tablespoon white wine vinegar
juice of $^1/_4$ lemon
salt
350ml good quality vegetable oil

Using an electric mixer, whisk the yolks, mustard, vinegar, lemon juice and salt. With the mixer running, add the oil in a thin stream. When half of the oil has been incorporated, pour in a thicker stream. Add a little more lemon juice if necessary and adjust the seasoning. Refrigerate, covered.

Balsamic Vinaigrette

(from page 74)

100g balsamic vinegar (preferably Modena, aged 4 years)
175ml extra virgin olive oil
1 tablespoon wholeseed mustard
$^1/_4$ red onion, peeled and finely diced
salt and white pepper to taste

Mix together all the ingredients (do not overmix).

Nahm Jim

(from page 78)

3 large red chillies, deseeded
1 bird's eye chilli
2 cloves garlic, peeled
3 coriander roots, scraped and cleaned
60g palm sugar, shaved
60ml fish sauce
140ml fresh lime juice

Pound the chillies, garlic and coriander roots with a mortar and pestle until an even paste is formed. Add the palm sugar, pound, then add the fish sauce and lime juice. The dressing should have an even balance between sweet, salty, hot and sour. Adjust if necessary.

Vegetable Stock

(from page 88)

2 large carrots, chopped
1 large onion, peeled and chopped
3 medium-large celery stalks, chopped
1 bay leaf
1 tablespoon chopped thyme
1 teaspoon freshly ground black pepper
salt to taste
2 litres water

Place all the ingredients in a saucepan. Simmer for 45 minutes over low heat. Cool then strain.

Watercress and Ginger Sauce

(from page 144)

1 bunch spinach leaves
1 bunch watercress, stems discarded
1cm fresh ginger, peeled and chopped
3 shallots
75ml chicken stock
salt to taste

Blanch and refresh the spinach, watercress and ginger. Purée in a blender with the shallots and chicken stock. Season with a little salt.

Pickle for Mushrooms

(from page 144)

1 cup Chinese white vinegar
½ cup water
⅓ cup sugar
1 slice fresh ginger, crushed
1 red chilli, halved
1 clove garlic, peeled and crushed
16 shiitake mushrooms, cleaned
salt

Mix together all the ingredients except the mushrooms and leave to infuse for half a day. Five minutes before serving, drop the mushrooms into the pickling solution. Remove and drain on kitchen paper. Season with a little salt.

Pasta Dough

(from page 156)

50g fine semolina
25g hard (bread) flour
2 egg yolks
5ml goose fat

Combine all the ingredients in a bowl and mix with a bread paddle for 20 minutes. Wrap in plastic cling film and allow to rest overnight.

Roll out the dough using a pasta machine set to Number 1, then cut out four 8cm rounds and four 10cm rounds.

Chocolate Sorbet

(from page 172)

500ml milk
500ml water
300g caster sugar
100g glucose
400g unsweetened chocolate

Bring the milk, water, caster sugar and glucose to the boil. Gradually stir in the chocolate until combined.

Chill and churn in an ice cream machine according to the manufacturer's instructions.

Clarified Butter

(from page 173)

To make clarified butter, melt unsalted butter in a heavy-based saucepan and simmer until it separates and the solids sink to the bottom of the pan. Ladle the clear liquid through a fine sieve into a container. Clarified butter can be refrigerated for weeks.

Roast Eschallots

(from page 188)

18 eschallots, skin on
milk
red wine vinegar
salt and freshly ground black pepper

Place the eschallots in a saucepan and cover with milk. Simmer for 20 minutes. Strain. Preheat the oven to 185°C. Place the eschallots in an oven dish lined with baking paper. Cover with tinfoil and roast for 20 minutes. Season with a splash of red wine vinegar, and salt and pepper.

Glossary

Bain marie
A large pan containing hot water in which a smaller pan may be set to cook food slowly or to keep food warm.

Brik pastry
Originating in Tunisia, this paper-thin pastry is similar to spring roll pastry but is not quite as pliable or stretchy.

Cavolo nero
The Italian name for Tuscan kale, green in colour and with a tangy bite that leaves an almost sweet aftertaste.

Chestnut mushrooms
A flavourful brown mushroom popular in Europe and Asia, similar to Portabello mushrooms.

Deglaze
Making a sauce by adding a small amount of liquid (wine, stock, lemon juice etc) to a pan that has small amounts of flavour-rich browned food particles stuck to it.

Dosa batter
Made from lentils and rice blended with water and left to ferment overnight.

Dragon fruit
Native to Central and South America and also known as pitaya, this stunningly beautiful fruit has an intense colour and shape, and a delicious taste.

Duck Maryland
The joint comprising the leg and thigh meat.

Durum wheat flour
Milled from hard-grain durum wheat, this flour is quite yellow in colour compared with regular flour and has a high gluten content, making it ideal for pasta.

Enoki mushrooms
These mushrooms have long, slender white stems, with tiny caps and grow in small clusters on live or dead tree trunks. They have a mild, delicate flavour and are used extensively in Asian cooking.

Escallops
A thin slice of meat (usually veal, e.g. the cut used for wiener schnitzel) usually fried or grilled.

Eschallots
Often confused with spring onions and also known as golden shallots, French shallots, khan kho (Vietnamese) and bawang merah (Indonesian/Malaysian) eschallots or shallots are composed of a number of onions attached to each other and have tubular leaves like a standard onion, but which are shorter and thinner. The tropical Asian shallot has a purplish skin with a pinkish interior.

Foie gras
The enlarged liver from a goose or duck that has been force-fed and fattened. After the bird is killed, the liver is soaked overnight in milk, water or port before being drained and then marinated.

Fried shallots
When fresh, these are normally purplish-red in colour. In their dried form they are freely available from Asian food stores and are ideal for sprinkling on salads.

Gai lan
Also known as Chinese Broccoli, this vegetable has glossy, blue-green leaves and crisp thick stems.

Harissa
A fiery red paste originating in Tunisia featuring chillies and a combination of garlic, caraway seeds, coriander seeds, cumin seeds, paprika, salt and olive oil. Use sparingly.

Kecap manis
Soy sauce sweetened with palm sugar and usually seasoned with garlic and star anise.

Katafi pastry
Shredded filo dough from Greece and the Middle East, usually used in the making of sweet desserts.

Kipfler potatoes
Waxy German finger potatoes.

Lardons
Small pieces of fatty bacon, usually cubed.

Lachsschinken
Smoked pork loin from Bavaria that has been dry-cured. When serving, it is thinly sliced similar to prosciutto.

Lotus root
Similar texture to water chestnut, i.e. crisp and fresh. Also available canned from Asian food stores.

Microgreens
Seedlings of various vegetables and greens, which are generally harvested after they form their first true leaves. Colourful and flavourful, they make a great garnish or an excellent salad.

Mirin
Sweet rice wine with a relatively low alcohol content used mostly in Japanese-style cuisine.

Mizuna leaves
Feathery, delicate Japanese salad vegetable with a distinct mustard flavour.

Morello cherries
An acidic and somewhat sour fruit, making it ideal for culinary purposes, native to much of Europe and south-west Asia.

Pomegranate molasses
A traditional ingredient in Middle Eastern cooking made from cooked-down pomegranate juice.

Ponzu vinegar
A blend of citrus juice, vinegar and other natural flavours. Makes a perfect marinade for grilled fish and poultry.

Porcini powder
Highly aromatic mushrooms, popular in Italian cuisine, dried and crumbled.

Quenelles
Oval-shaped dumplings made by shaping the mixture with two spoons. Also the name of the decorative shape made by shaping a mixture this way.

Rice paddy herb leaves
Available from specialist Asian food stores, these herbs are Vietnamese in origin.

Salsiccia
An Italian pork sausage that is not smoked or cured and which must be cooked before eating.

Semi-dried tomatoes
Softer and juicier than dried tomatoes, these are usually slow roasted in extra virgin oil.

Shaoxing
Chinese rice wine, used mostly for cooking, and named after a city in the Zhejiang Province of China.

Shiitake mushrooms
Native to East Asia, and also known as Chinese black mushroom and black forest mushrooms, they have many uses in Chinese and Japanese cuisines, especially in miso soup, as the basis for a kind of vegetarian dashi, and also as an ingredient in many steamed and simmered dishes.
If purchased dried, rehydrate by soaking in water before using.

Shimeji mushrooms
Also known as oyster mushrooms, they have delicate, sweet flesh with a nutty flavour and are suitable for stir-frying and pan-frying.

Smoked tomatoes
Tomatoes prepared in a smoker, which imparts a delicious flavour.

Sumac
A spice made from the dried powdered berries of the *Rhus coriaria* shrub, commonly used in Middle Eastern dishes.

Tahini
A paste made from ground hulled sesame seeds mixed with a little oil; a standard ingredient in the preparation of hummus.

Tamarind paste
Often sold compressed in blocks and consisting of the pulp surrounding the seeds of the tamarind pod, tamarind paste is used in a number of Asian dishes, including Thai-style traditional sour soup.

Tempura flour
Containing wheat flour, cornstarch, baking powder, and egg white, tempura flour is used to coat vegetables or seafood before deep-frying.

Verjuice
Acid liquid obtained from unripe fruit, especially grapes, often used in modern recipes for deglazing purposes.

Vanilla paste
A very popular flavouring available in paste form as well as the more common extract, vanilla paste is very concentrated and features the characteristic 'speckled pepper' appearance produced by the seeds themselves.

Yellow rock sugar
Known also as lump sugar, yellow rock sugar or rock candy, this is a solidified mixture of honey, refined and unrefined sugar.

Restaurant Directory

QUEENSLAND

Absynthe Restaurant, Shop 4 Q1 Gold Coast Highway, Surfers Paradise 4217, Ph: (07) 5504 6466

Butter Bistro, Corner Goodwin and Rotherham, Kangaroo Point, Brisbane 4006, Ph: (07) 3891 7005

Chill on Tedder Dining and Wine Bar, Shop 10/26, Tedder Ave, Main Beach 4217, Ph: (07) 5528 0388

Era Bistro, 100 Melbourne Street, South Brisbane 4101, Ph: (07) 3832 4722

Harvey's Restaurant, 4/31 James Street, Brisbane 4006, Ph: (07) 3852 3700

James Street Bistro, 39 James Street Fortitude Valley, Brisbane 4006, Ph: (07) 3852 5155

Joseph's Fine Dining & Supper, 471 Adelaide Street, Brisbane 4000, Ph: (07) 3839 2727

Mangostin's Restaurant, 65 The Esplanade, Cairns 4870, Ph: (07) 4031 9888

Pier Nine, 1 Eagle Street, Brisbane 4001, Ph: (07) 3226 2100

Red Ochre Grill, 43 Shields Street, Cairns 4870, Ph: (07) 4051 0100

Salsa Bar & Grill, 26 Wharf Street, Port Douglas 4877, Ph: (07) 4099 4922

NORTHERN TERRITORY

Kuniya Restaurant, Sails in the Desert Hotel, Yulara Drive, Ayers Rock Resort 0872, Ph: (08) 8957 7888

Pee Wee's at the Point, Alec Fong Lim Drive, East Point Reserve, Darwin 0801, Ph: (08) 8981 6868

WESTERN AUSTRALIA

Blue Water Grill, Duncraig Road, Applecross, Perth 6153, Ph: (08) 9482 0101

Fraser's Restaurant, Fraser Ave, Kings Park, West Perth 6005, Ph: (08) 9482 0104

Friends Restaurant, Hyatt Centre, 20 Terrace Road, East Perth 6004, Ph: (08) 9221 0885

Galileo Buona Cucina, 199 Onslow Road, Shenton Park, Perth 6008, Ph: (08) 9382 3343

Jackson's Restaurant, 483 Beafort Street, Highgate, Perth 6003, Ph: (08) 9328 1177

Star Anise, 225 Onslow Road, Shenton Park, Perth 6008, Ph: (08) 9381 9811

Subiaco Hotel, 465 Hay Street, Subiaco, Perth 6904, Ph: (08) 9381 3069

SOUTH AUSTRALIA

Appellation Restaurant, at Peppers the Louise, Seppeltsfield Road, Tanunda 5352, Ph: (08) 8562 4144

Capriccio Italian Restaurant, 10 Sussex Street, Glenelg, Adelaide 5045, Ph: (08) 8295 6453

Cos Restaurant, 18 Leigh Street, Adelaide 5000, Ph: (08) 8231 7644

Grange Restaurant, Hilton Adelaide, 233 Victoria Square, Adelaide 5000, Ph: (08) 8217 2000

Jolleys Boathouse, 1 Jolleys Lane, Adelaide 5000, Ph: (08) 8223 1739

Magill Estate Restaurant, 78 Penfold Road, Magill 5072, Ph: (08) 8301 5551

Salopian Inn, Cnr Willunga Road and McMurtrie Road, McLaren Vale 5171, Ph: (08) 8323 8769

TASMANIA

Blue Skies Café Restaurant & Bar, Ground Floor, Murray Street Pier, Hobart 7000, Ph: (03) 6224 3747

Tricycle Café Bar, Salamanca Art Centre, 71 Salamanca Place, Hobart 7001, Ph: (03) 6223 7228

VICTORIA

Antica Gelateria Del Corso, 161 Collins Street, Melbourne 3000, Ph: (03) 9654 5338

Grossi Florentino Restaurant, 80 Burke Street, Melbourne, Ph: (03) 9662 1811

Interlude, 211 Brunswick Street, Fitzroy, Melbourne 3065, Ph: (03) 9415 7300

Mecca, MR1, Mid Level Southgate, South Bank, Melbourne 3006, Ph: (03) 9682 2999

Montalto Vineyard and Olive Grove, 33 Shoreham Rd, Red Hill South 3937, Ph: (03) 5989 8412

Punch Lane Wine Bar and Restaurant, 43 Little Burke Street, Melbourne 3000, Ph: (03) 9639 4944

Quaff Restaurant, 436 Toorak Road, Toorak, Melbourne 3142, Ph: (03) 9827 4484

Souk, 267 Chapel Street, Prahran, Melbourne 3181, Ph: (03) 9533 7022

Three, One, Two, 312 Drummond Street, Carlton, Melbourne 3053, Ph: (03) 9347 3312

AUSTRALIAN CAPITAL TERRITORY

Mecca Bah, 25–29 Manuka Terrace, Minders Way, Manuka, Canberra 2603, Ph: (02) 6260 6700

The Boat House by the Lake, Grevillea Park, Menindee Drive, Barton, Canberra 2600, Ph: (02) 6273 5500

NEW SOUTH WALES

Bathers Pavilion, 4 The Esplanade, Balmoral Beach, Sydney 2088, Ph: (02) 9969 5050

La Grande Bouffe, 758 Darling Street, Rozelle, Sydney 2039, Ph: (02) 9818 4333

Manta Restaurant, The Wharf Woolloomooloo, 6 Cowper Wharf Road, Sydney 2011, Ph: (02) 9332 3822

The Boathouse on Blackwattle Bay, end of Ferry Road, Glebe, Sydney 2037, Ph: (02) 9518 9011

Yellow Bistro and Food Store, 57–59 Macleay Street, Potts Point, Sydney 2011, Ph: (02) 9357 3400

Artists, Agents and Outlets

(in alphabetical order, by artist, followed by page number)

Recipe Index